Praise for
A Radical Approach
to the Akashic Records

"For readers on the trajectory of Self-Realization, Melissa's experience, depth of knowledge, and process of ascending to higher levels of consciousness offers the opportunity for personal expansion. Regularly using the tools, techniques, and practices she shares assists one mastering their energy and raising their vibration to a frequency of Oneness and Love!"

—Linda Roebuck, MA, Counseling Psychology, Usui and Karuna Reiki Master
www.lindaroebuck.com

"What I love about this book is that it takes heady material and makes it accessible and easy to digest without compromising the depth of what is being discussed. Also, I found the content assisted me in feeling more empowered and intentional with my spiritual practice."

—Lisanne Cormier, L.Ac

"I've been lucky enough to know Melissa Feick for a decade and have experienced her as a mentor, teacher, and friend. This book captures her life's work in a way that's easy to understand and implement. Melissa expertly shares her substantial knowledge with humor and insight as she relays cases studies and client examples, so the reader never feels overwhelmed. Whether you're new to metaphysical work or more advanced, A Radical Approach to the Akashic Records gives a fresh perspective of an ancient tool. A must addition to your Akashic Records library!"

—Diane L Haworth, Spiritual Coach, Speaker & Author
www.DianeHaworth.com

"Melissa is many things: a teacher, an intuitive, a friend, a thinker, a mother, a woman, an explainer, a counselor, a healer, but mostly she is a way shower. If you let her show you the way your spiritual evolution will take a quantum leap and you will fulfill the reason you came here this time."

—Phil Brentwood, Author *Are You God?*

"Melissa has given her readers an opportunity and methodology to expand to their highest soul potential in this lifetime. I found this book immensely thorough in describing the process of accessing the Akashic Records and transcending Karma. Thank you for composing this Divine strategy to assist the world to unwind back to peace, love, joy, and unity."

—Michelle Lightworker, Exec. Producer, FiveD.tv-Director, Lightworker Foundation Ltd www.lightworkerfoundation.org

"A Radical Approach to the Akashic Records is a breath of fresh air and insight. While it is practical and grounded, it is also immensely deep and rich, taking the reader on both an inner and ascending journey where we have access to the most highly impactful and life-altering shifts."

—Katy Bray co-founder, Lead with the Lights On www.LeadwiththeLightsOn.com

A Radical Approach to the
AKASHIC RECORDS

Master Your Life and Raise Your Vibration

SPIRITUAL EXPANSION
PUBLISHING

Melissa Feick

Founder of the Spiritual Expansion Academy

Cover design and illustration: Heidi Sutherlin, My Creative Pursuits

ISBN: 1-7325393-6-7
ISBN-13: 978-1-7325393-6-5

Download
5 Ways to Raise Your Vibration Now!

Free eBook with great information about the Law of Vibration and how to raise your vibrational frequency immediately!

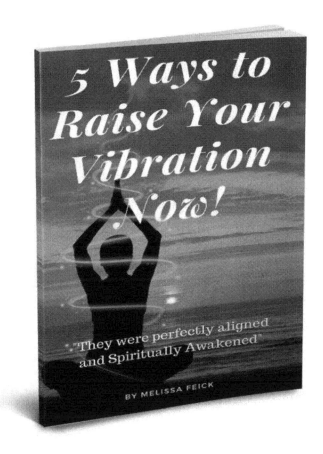

Here is a fantastic way to raise your vibrational frequency immediately!

Download this FREE eBook today!

https://melissafeick.com/raise-vib-ebook/

To my children Connor and Kyra: I am amazed by your open hearts and your desire to be of service! Thank you for choosing me as your mother, it has been and continues to be a privilege.

CONTENTS

Exercises

Thank You!

This book comes from a place of love and service! I am so grateful for every being who has entered my life in one way or another. I see the perfection of all my relationships and the beauty of the world!

The most influential people in my life are my amazing Father and Mother, Jim and Betty Martin. You taught me the importance of faith while instilling the love of inquisitiveness. I love you more than you could ever understand, and I am the luckiest person alive to have such loving parents!

I am grateful to my two beautiful children, Connor and Kyra: you've listened to me talk about energy your whole lives, and you still love me! I love you with all my heart!

Thank you, Lane, for all your support and love. You've been a great dad and husband, and I'm so grateful that you were open enough to help me pursue my interest in spirituality.

To my sisters Terry, Carol, and Roe: We are the mighty Martin Clan! Thanks for all your support and love!

I also want to thank my amazing friend, Sofia Wren, who lovingly guided me in editing this book and gave me great advice with a sharp eye for detail! And to my friend Taryn Ryan for reading through the entire book twice to find mistakes.

To all my students in my Ascension class: Val, Diana, Don, Lisanne, Laura H., Laura L., Jennifer, Tracy, Phil, Linda, April, Dori, Aimee, Taryn, Sharka, and Angela: You guys rock! You've supported me in so many ways and I'm so grateful to have each of you in my life!

I am also blessed to have some wonderful connections with so many of my clients, students, and friends! This book is part of my journey I had because of you!

And to my buddy and partner in all things spiritual, Diane Haworth: You have guided me, kicked me in the ass, but most of all made me laugh so hard I've almost peed my pants several times! You are my sounding board and best friend. Thanks for being there through all the phone calls about this book!

INTRODUCTION

You've been called to serve and create a transformation. The world needs you.

You are aware that the world needs more of us to be in the space of love and connection together. Perhaps you've always known this, or maybe it's just starting to be evident to you now.

You are ready for a change, right now. You've got a deep desire to transform and become your highest vibrational potential because you want healthy, happy relationships, both with yourself and others.

You have a special purpose on the planet, but you aren't alone in this. It's not just you. There is a radical spiritual awakening happening all over the world. The Akashic Records say that the intention of the shift is to transform the overstimulated lower energies like anger, hatred, and struggle. It is time for these stuck lower energies to transform into something higher, for all of us. How do you know this? By the very fact that you are here on the planet now. Are you ready to take part in this healing process, starting with healing yourself?

This book contains radical information about the Akashic Records. Much of this information builds on an ancient understanding of the Akashic Records, with new insight only recently discovered. This new accelerated spiritual awakening urges us to take a fresh approach to the Records and our evolution as conscious beings. The material I present on Karma will teach you the real secret to transformation. With this information, you'll be excited to go deeper into the Records and to discover the ease of creating real shifts in your life and the lives of others. This transformation is moving those old stuck feelings into a higher vibration: expansive, spiraling energy of creation.

The Radical Approach to the Akashic Records is one of the best *ascension* tools available to humans to date. Many of us get stuck in the wheel of cause and effect: we tend to recreate our past hurts and traumas. While you're transforming in the Records, you will allow your past to heal, and as a result, you will change by transcending that Karma, which also will change the world. The Records are an amazing tool because most people do not master the limits of the mental mind by just thinking nor do they master their past emotional traumas by reliving the trauma. The best way to master these things is to release the energy connected to it, and the best way to do this release work is through the Akashic Records. In this book, you will learn a simple, easy process of reaching the Akashic Records on the Quantum Field so that you may transcend the lower vibrations and create a life filled with Joy!

Perhaps something has changed to shake you awake recently, or maybe you've been doing this work for some time. As an awakened person you understand the need to raise your vibration or energy. You know that you'll be happier and more confident this way. One of the easiest and fastest ways to raise your vibration and to be more joyful is to spend time in the Akashic Records. When you are spending time in the Records having experiences—giving or receiving readings, healings, meditating and creating—you will be able to start manifesting all that you desire and more. You will experience manifestation at the highest potential, which will expand your understanding and compassion towards yourself and others.

On the Physical Plane, you tend to see the world linearly since we all perceive time and space with a beginning and an end, as part of our sensory experience. This linear concept, however, is part of the illusion of this plane of existence. The illusion of time and space doesn't need to entangle you in that reality anymore.

The Akashic Records will allow you to see beyond the illusion and the linear belief of time and space. This illusion of limitation is what creates all your feelings of lack, scarcity, and fear. To step outside of that illusion is how you can connect to your true power to create how you want to feel. Throughout this book, take notice of concepts that may be new to you, like the spiral energy found in the Quantum Field, in the levels of existence and in the Akashic Records. We will use the spiral energy as an analogy of the healing and manifesting within the Records that connects you to your true joyful self.

In this book, you will learn the fastest way to transcend the illusion and master the lower self. This book is inspired in part by Ascended Masters. The Ascended Masters are "ascended" because they mastered and ascended past the lower planes where many humans struggle. They also ascended and mastered the physical, emotional and mental bodies where many people feel scarcity or pain. The Ascended Masters have been where you and I are now, ready to transcend! You can learn how to master your reality as well, by tapping into their wisdom and the Records.

All humans are on this planet to *master* the physical, emotional and mental bodies, as well as the physical, emotional and mental levels. The Records will help you create deep changes so you may master the bodies and levels. When you start working in the Records, you will understand the depth of the healing that can happen, which will help you and others to experience profound inner transformation.

This book came from Divine inspiration and years of meditation and study. The information flows easily and is interconnected for ease of understanding and enables you to reach higher states of consciousness.

It might surprise you, but the real benefit of connecting with the Akashic Records on the Quantum Field is that you will become accustomed to being in a frequency of Oneness and Love. You'll come to understand why working in the Akashic Records on the level of the Quantum Field is so different. This connection to Oneness and Love can be the foundation to everything you do as a conscious spiritual being. You can integrate it into things you already do, as well as things you learn in the future. You can use it in your Reiki or other healing modalities, you can use it to do readings for yourself or clients, and you can use it to do some deep transformational work on yourself or others.

This book is just the beginning of your higher frequency connection. There are no limits to using this book, just as there are no limitations to using the Records. You can use the instructions provided over and over again to transform different areas of your life and also work with others to help them transform, as well. The information and the meditations in this book will blow you away, so get ready to raise your vibration and transform your life!

The best part of what I'm going to teach you about the Akashic Records is how to connect to the Records on the Quantum Field. When you are one with the Quantum Field in the Records, you can change and recreate anything that is not working in your life. You can deal with family issues, illness, fear, money stress, and emotional or mental turmoil about anything. I'm going to show you how to do this, and it's so easy! I mean so easy, anyone can be taught how to do this healing process. My clients, students and I have used this method of connecting to the Records to accomplish some profound healing that results in manifesting real-life changes very quickly.

To show you just how powerful these techniques are, I'll give you an example. As I was doing a reading and healing in the Records for a client who works as a healer, I saw entangled patterns in her Records which were connected to her absorbing energy from other people, like her family and clients. She would allow the energy of other people into her body due to her past lives as a shaman. When she was a shaman, she took on the energy of the sick. She also experienced this entangled pattern in this lifetime because of childhood abuse she had experienced. She then took on the energy of her family, habitually, to protect herself, to stay safe, and to feel needed and loved. The client realized that this pattern was no longer helping her or helping her to feel her best. As we were in the Records, we healed and cleared the energy around these unhelpful patterns, and alongside this, we healed the other issues around a belief that taking on other people's energy was her purpose.

She realized the real reason for her pattern was that she was only taking on other people's energy because she needed to feel loved and special. Since it affected her adversely, she didn't want to continue that anymore. She found clarity and healing in the Records, and she was finally able to let all of that go.

Luckily, this isn't a mystical book that will talk about mystical experiences and leave you wanting more. You won't end up yearning for those higher experiences and then end the book not knowing how to access them for yourself. No way! This book is a step by step guide, giving you the 'what, why and how' of achieving mystical experiences through the Akashic Records.

It is important that you utilize the Akashic Records in a way that will transform your life. You can't connect with the Akashic Records and get the deepest and most profound shifts without knowing what the

Akashic Records are, what they can do for you, and how to use them for the greatest healing. We will start with what the Akashic Records are and what to do while in the Records. You'll learn everything you need to know to access the Records on the deepest level.

You can create an amazing life of manifestation and creation by going into your Records and healing all past issues or Karma. It is one of the simplest and most profound methods of healing and enlightenment.

You are not destined to live a life of pain and sorrow! You are not here to be angry or to feel unloved and underappreciated. You are here for a greater experience. Yes, I said 'experience!' You are here to experience the mystical energy of pure consciousness while being here on Earth.

This book includes meditations and exercises. My suggestion is to read each chapter and do the meditation or exercise as you go along. They are the foundation you will need to read the Akashic Records on the Quantum Field. You can also go into the Akashic Records to process things related to what you read in each chapter, like exploring your Karma when you read Chapters Seven and Eight on Karma.

This isn't just a book; it's a workbook!

When you get to places in the book where there are meditations, you can either read through the meditations and do them on your own or download each meditation from my website.[1]

There is no right or wrong way to utilize your Records. The way I will teach you is simple and powerful. The more time you spend in the Records, the stronger your connection with the Akashic Records will be.

---

[1] https://melissafeick.com/rar-meditations/

You will also be more comfortable and able to receive more profound healings.

Many see the Akashic Records as a way to access your past lives, but they are so much more than that. Although it's possible to learn about past lives through accessing the Records, the Akashic Records have a greater purpose: to help you transcend the human existence and live life more consciously. The Records are not just to be used to find the negative, that is to find out what is wrong in your life. The Records can help connect you to your gifts, the positive Karma, and the truth of your soul essence.

You may find yourself experiencing natural changes in your life. Remember that working with the Akashic Records can smooth the ride of your transformation so that it can feel as good and easy as possible. The only way out is through the Records. If you are reading this book, then you know that there is more potential for your life and you are ready to be all of who you truly are. If you do the work throughout the book, you will discover so many hidden gems in the Records to help you pursue this aim. This step by step process will also help you feel comfortable reading the Akashic Records for others. Follow this process, and you are sure to enjoy your transformation from those lower energies that have long existed in the world, and your life personally, into a bright future filled with awakening and unconditional Love.

Most of all have fun and enjoy!

-Melissa Feick

Chapter 1

Soul Purpose

The process of accessing the Akashic Records begins with you. I tell all of my students who want to learn how to read the Records to set their intention before they begin. But let's back up a moment before you dive into the Records. What is your intention for being here, on the planet? What is your Soul Purpose?

The misconception of a Soul Purpose in the spiritual community is that the Soul has come here to do something important. Many assume that Soul Purpose and life purpose are similar. The idea of life purpose is that, as humans, we came here with a specific mission to *do* something. When we don't *do* our mission then that will mean we will always be unhappy, our life will suck, and our soul will keep begging us to *do* what we came here *to do.* That way of thinking about things is so detrimental to spiritual seekers. The truth is that your life purpose is about how you live your life and how you express your Soul Purpose. **Soul Purpose isn't about the doing; it's about *being*.**

Your Soul Purpose is to *Be* more in alignment with who you truly are. *Be connected. Be compassion.* What and how you express this *beingness* is the key to 'living your life purpose.' You can be a cashier at a small town grocery store and be living your life purpose.

Your Soul Purpose is in direct alignment with your life purpose. You can't have one without the other; they have the same vibration, so they are a vibrational match. The spiritual community emphasizes that everyone's Soul Purpose is different, i.e., this guy's purpose is to be a writer, and the other a teacher. What about the idea that we have many purposes, and that narrowing it down to one will disconnect the soul from his or her purpose? Since your Soul Purpose and life purpose are aligned, your ultimate purpose on Earth is to *be*, not do! The *doing* aspect is one part of how we express and experience our soul self.

The reason so many people are unhappy in their jobs, or in their lives, is that they aren't listening to their soul's voice. Your soul is conveying how to be more in alignment with your Soul Purpose, and how you express this is through *being*ness, not what you are doing. You express your beingness by being what you want to see in the world. Oprah is a good example of someone who expresses her soul's beingness. Her Soul Purpose wasn't to be a talk show host; her purpose was in alignment with being a vessel of sharing her wisdom. How she chose to do that did not matter as much. Your soul wants you to express *who* you are being, which is more important than what you are doing! Oprah is *being* the change and expressing that in so many ways. She is living her purpose through being a public figure for the spiritual evolution. Oprah has the innate ability to be a teacher and a leader; she could have done that in many ways. We have innate abilities, but that isn't about our Soul Purpose.

The next statement will rock your boat... **everyone's, and yes, I mean** *everyone's*, **Soul Purpose is the same.** Holy Sh*t. How does this work?

What do I mean? Did I boggle your mind? Did that psychic tell you that your purpose was to be a healer, to save the Earth, to work with dolphins or children?

Ok, I know the suspense is too much. Do you want to know what your true Soul Purpose is? **Everyone's Soul Purpose is to transcend the illusion and the ego's delusion, to express Love, and to become the energy of equanimity.** I'm sure that sounds easy, right?

You are here to recognize the illusion which, in turn, teaches you how to *take responsibility* for your creations and to learn to create what you desire, instead of creating all the crap in your life. Why would your soul come all the way here from its nice resting place to learn something so simple yet so complex? You are here to master the lower planes of existence, and once you recognize that this plane is an illusion, and master the planes, you have completed what you came here to do.

Once you recognize the illusion, you become happier, and you experience more inner joy, inner peace, the feelings of Oneness and Expansion, to name a few. These are the higher states of consciousness which is your soul essence. When you wrap yourself in the blanket of shame, guilt, sadness, or anger, and see the world as a dark place and see the people of the Earth as bad, then you are *buying into the illusion*. Buying into the illusion keeps you stuck in the fear, anger, and guilt.

When you start to recognize that you are living in an illusion and that there is no right or wrong, good or bad, you will learn to forgive, and let go of the anger and sadness. Most of the people who've had near-death experiences will tell you that this world is not real and that you are not a victim of the Earth. After their death, they come back with a feeling of peace, love, and connection. They experienced the truth, wouldn't you like to experience that now?

If this is pushing an emotional button for you, or you're having an internal argument about the time when someone hurt you, and how real it is, or how it was real when a bad situation happened to you, please take a breath. Yes, that was a terrible thing, but it does not need to be a story that you hold onto for lifetimes. You'll learn more about the illusion throughout the later chapters, especially Chapter Seven.

Please know that letting go of pain is not about believing or telling others that this world is an illusion. The true transformation happens when you no longer see the world in an angry, sad or bitter way. You start to perceive what happens to yourself and others with compassion and love. You see the bigger picture, and you are less likely to want to fight, argue, or withdraw. You know that you're transforming when you see through the illusion, and you feel equanimity when you encounter something that *used* to upset you.

Equanimity is a term Buddhists use when they are connecting compassion and feeling neutral about a situation or event. Equanimity is when you feel love and compassion while in the middle of a chaotic situation.

You'll be using the Records to do all these things for yourself and others. When you go into the Akashic Records to do a reading for your clients or yourself, you want to be able to see the patterns that are holding back their highest potential.

SOUL LESSONS

When I first studied spiritual concepts in the 90's, I would hear all this talk about lessons and how important it is for us to learn lessons. When something difficult or upsetting happened, my teachers would ask, "What lesson did you learn from that?" or "What is the lesson in that situation?" One day I was working with a client, and she was telling me about the lesson she was supposed to learn from a difficult situation in her life. My guides started telling me that it didn't have to be a difficult lesson to learn. Everything that happens in your life is *just an experience,* and it's the energy you put into that experience that makes it either a difficult or negative experience, a neutral experience, or a positive experience.

Every moment you are choosing whether to see a situation in one of three ways: positive, negative or neutral. If a man walks up to a group of three people, and tells them a short story and walks away, they will all have different reactions. Why is that? Each person is coming from their perspective. The first person will say he was an asshole; the second person will say he was hysterical; the third person will say he was boring. They all see this person differently.

Have you ever heard someone tell you a story about the lesson they were learning or had to learn? It's usually negative. Why don't we ever have positive lessons? I've never had a client or friend tell me that the lesson they learned was amazing. I'm waiting for someone to tell me that they had to learn a lesson about winning the lottery and finding the soul mate of their dreams. Or that their amazing lesson is about moving to an exotic land they've always wanted to live, and now they have time and money to travel and live the life of their dreams every moment.

We tend to call negative experiences lessons, but they are only experiences. These experiences upset you, and when we use the word lesson, it makes you feel like there is a right way or a wrong way to handle the situation like you had control over the situation. For instance, "I've learned my lesson to stay away from her." Next time you come across a lesson, take a look at what's happening, and what you can understand about yourself and your reaction. *It's more about self-realization and less about the lesson.*

In Chapters Seven and Eight, we will get deep into the real meaning of Karma. You'll learn how the idea of lessons and Karma can help you transcend the limitations of the world and discover the higher understanding of who you truly are.

Self-Realization

Part of discovering the illusion and what illusion means comes from the important concept of self-realization. I first heard this term when I studied Paramahansa Yogananda's Self-Realization Fellowship in the early 2000's. I loved the idea of meditation and the way he aligned meditation into a daily practice to self-realization.

Self-realization means the fulfillment of one's potential, and the potential of the soul self, or the higher consciousness. I feel that knowing oneself so intimately is the key to self-realization and that personal development and the spiritual journey are some of the *best tools* to understand all aspects of yourself.

If you take a look around you, you see people who are always in reactionary mode. They're just reacting and have no idea what they are doing or why they do it. They're living an *unconscious life.*

When you live a life of self-realization, you see the world through the eyes of your higher consciousness. You see the truth and the illusion at the same time. You recognize the true self of others and forgive easily.

When you live your life in self-realization, you start to take personal responsibility for all that you do without guilt or anger. You see things in a higher perspective, and the lessons become neutral experiences. You love more, and you laugh harder. You live in a state of the higher consciousness of bliss, self-love, inner joy and expansion.

Soul Purpose

You are here to become the higher states of consciousness, to connect with your true self and your divinity within. You're not here to talk about your purpose, to wish you were doing your purpose, or to wonder what your purpose is. You are here to be a human, to *transcend the lower ego self, to transcend your Karma, and become your higher consciousness.*

It is possible to work through your Karma and connect to your higher self through the use of the tools in this book. You will be using the Akashic Records in the Oneness Field (Quantum Field) to get an intimate understanding of your Karma or life path, to take responsibility, and to transcend any lower energies.

Your Soul Purpose is to transcend the illusion of the duality of this Universe, and an easy way to do this is to let go of old issues, or Karma, from this life and other lives, in the Akashic Records. Throughout this book, I help you raise your vibration and live the life you desire. Once you start to recognize the illusion and unwind your past, the higher states of consciousness start to become more present in your life. You'll feel less of the pain, anger, resentment, or guilt, and you no longer react to situations negatively. You will start to see both sides of the issue, and take responsibility for your side.

While on the Earth plane you are in this body and you want to be happy, right? You feel you have this weight that keeps you down; it may be the weight of old hurt and pain, or of the family that needs you to support them, or just a deep sadness or grief. Whatever it is, you can transcend it! You are in charge of your life, you are in charge of your creation, and it's time for you to start creating what you want.

CREATION

When you start taking responsibility for your creation, you take your power back! Take your power back today. You don't have to be perfect, start one day at a time. Once I teach you how to start working in the Akashic Records to unwind your past, and to be in the higher states of consciousness, you will understand that you have control over what happens to you in your life. The Akashic Records hold all potential or all possibilities, so you aren't just healing your past, you are also creating the life you desire.

You are not a victim of your current life or other lifetimes. You are the creator. Every moment you create your next moment by your thoughts and feelings. Don't give up on yourself. Take your power back and consciously create the life you desire.

When you live in the past, whether it's an experience from your past or a past life, you keep recreating the past. Many years ago I had a client who came to me for a reading. I don't remember the details of the reading but I know it was accurate and her guides gave her advice and tools to change some things in her life that was no longer working. About two years later, she came for another reading. In the middle of the reading, she said: "This is the same reading you gave me two years ago." I connected to my intuition to show me what was going on because it is unusual for me to do the same reading for anyone. My readings are always different because I bring through what is best for each client, and I am an advanced reader.

My guides said she hadn't changed anything; that she was still living in the past. I asked her, "What has changed in the last two years for the reading to change?" At first, she didn't understand the question. She didn't understand it because she was so unaware of herself and her life. She lived her life going through the motions but never taking responsibility to change her life. She wanted a different life but didn't do anything to make that happen.

She was creating the same life because she was creating from her past. She was creating the same family and coworkers, even if they had different names; they treated her the same, and she had the same experiences with them.

You have a choice to either create from your past or create a new experience and create an amazing future. It's time to start recognizing that you can create a better experience through using the Akashic Records for unwinding your past, gaining self-realization, and creating a more exciting future.

HOW TO BE IN A DOING UNIVERSE

I want to help you feel more empowered and less like a victim to your circumstances. I have spent years looking deeper into the pain and issues of my life and the lives of my clients. I know that it's possible to live your life *Being* who and what you came here to *Be*.

Being and doing are opposites, and if you want to transcend the lower vibrations, you will want to start to express your existence through Being. You will still do things, let's face it most of us still have to do laundry to have clean clothes. You can Be the energy of connection and Love while doing the laundry. The Being aspect is the Divine within, doing is human. You are both so you will want to do what you need to do in life while Being who you truly are.

The way to *Be* in a doing universe is to start to become more aware of both your individual patterns and your family patterns and to heal these patterns in the Akashic Records. You will need to look deeply at yourself and do the inner work. It's important to stop looking outside yourself to heal your wounds or to change. You are ready to take back your power and create inner transformation. Don't let your ego talk you out of this; it's worth the time and effort.

Once you see your experiences as a result of your creation, you will recognize how you can start to make major shifts within yourself and help your clients. You will start becoming the love, peace, and compassion you know is there. You will start *Being* who you are meant to *Be* and stop trying to *do* something to change your life. *You will start Being.*

SOUL TRANSCENDENCE

Your soul has come here to connect to who you truly are, but your experience on Earth has diluted that connection. It's time for you to transcend the lower illusions and the emotional and mental energy that keep you believing that you are here only as a human. You are ready to transcend the lower vibrations and connect to your higher consciousness.

As I said before, the easiest way to transcend and raise your vibration this is through the Akashic Records. In the next chapter, I will go into depth of how to get to the highest vibration of the Records. You will learn about the Universe and how the Planes of Existence are here to support your transition into becoming a higher vibration and mastering your life.

Chapter 2

Cosmology - Planes of Existence

In the first chapter, I stated that we all have the same purpose, to transcend the illusion and the ego's delusion, to express Love, and to become the energy of equanimity. The Planes of Existence can help you to transcend the illusion. As you move through the understanding of the planes, you will receive a great deal of insight into the illusion and how to reach the highest level of the Akashic Records.

You are a multidimensional being, and since you have the potential to connect with many dimensions it's empowering for you to understand how to interact with the different dimensions of the Planes of Existence! The Planes play an important role in our ability to reach the highest vibration of the Akashic Records. According to the works of great thinkers like Madame Blavatsky, the Upanishads, as well as modern physicists, we live in a multidimensional Universe with many different energies that are constantly interacting with each other. Since there are infinite dimensions that we are continually interacting, it's important for you to understand a little about the levels of existence which house the infinite dimensions around us all.

Each Plane of Existence that we are going to look at in this book houses infinite dimensions. As we move through the dimensions, we move through the planes. It is a symbiotic relationship.

The way I was shown to connect to the Akashic Records was to pass through the planes into the Quantum Field of Pure Divine Love or the Oneness Field. (It's difficult to know the name of the field, everyone calls it something different, but it's the essence of the Divine no matter what you call it.) Not everyone works on this level, but the difference it makes is powerful.

To transcend the illusion quickly, you will want to reach the highest level in the Akashic Records and to experience the major healing that comes along with that. It's essential to understand the cosmos and the planes to do that. And you must know what you are doing. What *are* you healing? You're healing the Physical, Emotional and Mental bodies within your energy system.

The three Physical, Emotional and Mental levels or planes of existence correspond to the three levels of our Physical, Emotional and Mental bodies. You came to the Earth to work on mastering the Physical, Emotional and Mental bodies so you may ascend *through* and master the Physical, Emotional and Mental planes and be in the Oneness of the Quantum Field.

In other words, *the planes of existence correspond to the states of human consciousness*, Mental, Emotional and Physical. Once you accept and utilize this connection between mastering the human energy system and mastering the planes of existence, you will experience massive transformation in your life!

LEVELS OF EXISTENCE

Many explain the planes of existence as a hierarchy which means that one plane is higher than the other. As humans, we see the world as linear, and it's easier for our rational mind to comprehend the planes as a hierarchy.

Many see the planes as having the Physical Plane on the bottom with the Emotional Plane above that and the Mental Plane above that. It is a simplistic model of the planes, and it makes sense since you see the world around you in this manner.

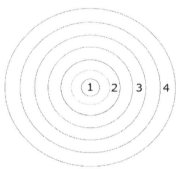

1: Physical Plane
2: Emotional Plane
3: Mental Plane
4: Quantum Field

We only need to understand the three planes which correspond with our human experience. All of these levels are complex and have infinite dimensions within them. These three planes also connect you to the cycle of rebirth and death (reincarnation) which keeps you focused on the illusion of this world.

On these lower planes, you are constantly experiencing duality. The energy of duality is part of the human experience in the lower planes, and the duality creates the feeling of isolation and separation. This separation shows up in your life through familiar patterns; us versus them, right versus wrong, good versus bad, anger versus love, and so on. This duality keeps you feeling attached to the illusion of the lower planes. If you are attached, you cannot ascend easily. *The lower planes connect to the illusion of hierarchy, duality, and time and space.*

In cosmology, the study of the cosmos, each plane or dimension exists within itself; there isn't a separation between the planes. This feeling and experience of separation or duality is a total deception since all the planes are connected and correspond to each other.

The illusion of separation is a concept all the mystics try to explain to us. Note how your mind finds it easy to buy into—but there is something more for you to discover and that is how you will master reality.

Instead of perceiving the planes as a hierarchy, think about it as a spiral within another spiral. Within this spiral are every dimension and plane. The planes are constantly interacting with and moving through each other. There isn't any separation within the planes; they are all part of each other, so the Physical Plane is part of the Mental and Emotional plane. It's like a spiral that is within one plane, which is within all the planes.

These planes spiral within each other, and they connect and correspond to each other. The planes interact energetically through this spiraling of energy. When you are caught up in the illusion, your experiences are linear, and you assume that time and space is also linear. That's the illusion we believe, that you are living in a linear environment and that one thing always happens after the other.

As long as you comprehend the basic knowledge of the planes and how duality influences your life, you'll be able to reach the Akashic Records on the Quantum Field. The beauty of working in the Akashic Records is that it can help you to master the lower planes and bodies so that you may disengage from the wheel of Karma and illusion.

In Chapters Seven and Eight you'll learn more in-depth information about Karma, but for now, understand that that Karma isn't about the concept of punishment or that you have to experience Karmic retribution. *Karma is much more enlightening and empowering than that.* Karma is about self-realization and transcending the illusion that keeps you connected to the lower planes.

The concept of linear time and space creates a false belief that what you did in the past (past Karma) is why you are experiencing illness and sadness now.

TIME AND SPACE

What you perceive as space is illusionary and what you perceive about time is a lie. Have you ever noticed that there are situations when time speeds up or slows down?

My first conscious memory of experiencing time slowing happened when I was about 11 years old. My older sister's friend was driving us home in the rain, and he was driving too fast over a bridge. Before I knew what was happening, we were starting to hydroplane. I remember that it seemed like the car was spinning in slow motion and time did not become normal until we hit the guardrail in an abrupt stop. It felt like we were spinning for a longer amount of time than we were. I asked my sister if she noticed that time slowed down and she didn't know what I meant. For years, I thought it was so cool how time slowed down at that moment. It wasn't until I learned about time and space as an illusion that I could see how significant that experience was for me.

I now understand time and the limiting beliefs about time. Sometimes I will see if I can get somewhere in a shorter amount of time than usual by intentionally bending time. If I hear clients or friends say that they don't have enough time, or that they wasted time, I try to help them understand that those words and energy affects how they experience time in their life. I suggest that they try to say instead, "I always have plenty of time" and "I don't need to rush," or "I'm always on time" instead of, "I'm always late."

Most people see life as a series of events and experiences which is an illusion. In truth, reality and everything you experience is happening at the same time and space all at once. It is up to you to call the illusion out and not to buy into it.

Since all the planes are interconnected, the Quantum Field or Oneness space, which is timeless and infinite in space, can be part of our experience here on the Earth plane. Since there isn't any time and space (Earthly space) in the Oneness, we can also experience timelessness and infinity while living in a body on the Earth.

Many years ago, it was customary for people to lie about their age all the time. My grandmother told everyone she was ten years younger than she was. When she died at age 91, we thought she was 81. She looked amazing for 81, let alone 91! She believed she was younger than her years on Earth. She believed she was young!

Since time is an illusion, space also has to be an illusion, since they are connected. I have a bunch of stories, both from my own life and from people I know, about items appearing in their space that were not there before. Yeah, things appearing out of nowhere!!!

Lauren, one of my clients, was coming home on a plane from Florida back to Maryland. On her vacation, she bought an organic jar of pickles. She loved pickles and was excited about her wonderful pickle purchase. At security, they stopped her and said she couldn't take her pickles on the plane. She understood and even though she was so happy about the pickles, she knew she had to let them go. The TSA agent took the jar out of her bag, placed the pickles with the other confiscated security paraphernalia and let Lauren go on her way to her gate.

Lauren proceeded to tell me that when she got in the car and rummaged through her bag—there were her pickles! There was no way the pickles were placed in her bag by a human; both she and her friend saw the TSA agent place the jar on the counter.

Since there is no space, things can appear and disappear, and this should be a normal experience. Paramahansa Yogananda followers tell stories of how different items would show up around him during meditation. He is the famous guru who wrote Autobiography of a Yogi. I have heard about many other master meditators that have shown us that time and space are an illusion and that things can appear and disappear.

CYCLE OF KARMA

Although you'll read more details about Karma in Chapters Seven and Eight, understanding the cycle or wheel of Karma is essential to your comprehension of the planes. I see your choice to incarnate on the Earth plane as part of a desire to experience creation on a dense level. This experience helps you evolve your consciousness. Here you can master and experience the duality of the Physical, Emotional and Mental planes and bodies. I see human beings coming to this plane as similar to taking an adventurous trip like hiking in the Alps! We all came here because we want to see and discover new things.

Spirit has told me that as we moved into this realm, we started to feel separate from Divine Love and we became caught up in the illusion of the linear, dualistic energy of the lower planes. You've spent lifetimes trapped in the linear experience, which makes you stuck within the cycle of Karma on the Earth plane. Since there is no time and space, this progression is all happening in an instant, so your infinite self is experiencing everything at once. Remember the spiral concept? Your purpose is to spiral your way upward toward your higher consciousness and disengage from the linear delusion as you transcend the illusion.

This linear experience of the Earth plane is an illusion, and if you buy into this illusion, as so many people do, you get duped into believing the illusion is real and you won't believe in miracles and the ability to create your reality. You'll see the world as absolutes. Absolute up and down, black and white, yes and no. This view of the world will result in making you feel very unhappy because you'll feel separate and alone. *There is no area of openness and possibilities when we see the world as absolute and dualistic.*

In reality, the world around you is made up of planes and dimensions that are constantly interacting with you. This interaction is happening spirally, and you are interacting and creating your reality through your thoughts and your emotions.

When you believe that the linear time and space are real, and you get caught up in the illusion of your stories of sadness and pain, that means your soul has not mastered that Physical, Emotional or Mental planes. Since you have not mastered those planes and bodies that means that you are caught up in the cycle of Karma.

Once you evolve your consciousness through working in the Akashic Records, you'll begin to master the lower planes. Through this mastery, you begin to see your experience more in the spiral energy and less linearly.

People keep incarnating on Earth because they believe in the illusion and, Karma and they get caught up in the feelings and stories from this Earth plane. You keep bringing back, into each incarnation, more energy from your past experiences. In each lifetime we all can move through the Karmic patterns that we came here to transcend, but it seems so many of us keep recreating these patterns. You can use the Akashic Records to work through your old story and the emotions that keep you stuck believing in the illusion of this world. While working in the Records, you have the opportunity to master the lower planes and be your higher consciousness.

The most exciting part is that at this moment there is a huge spiritual awakening because the energy is shifting to a higher frequency. The energy of hiding the ancient understanding of your life and your soul is clearly impossible. Any information you need to help you become more connected to your soul is at your fingertips. It's time for you to understand the connection between being a human being and transcending that illusion so that you can become more of who you truly are. Others have already been creating those very same miracles, so you know, on some level, that it is possible for you, too. When you start letting go of your past Karma in the Records, you will start to create miracles.

Also, when you are ready to provide readings in the Akashic Records for others, it will be best if you have the intention of helping them move past their Karmic ties to the lower planes so they can evolve. Chapter Twelve will help you do this.

THE PLANES OF EXISTENCE

As I mentioned earlier, the lower planes are part of our connection to the illusion. You came here to master these planes of existence and to transcend the limitation of your Physical, Emotional and Mental bodies.

I'll explain the lower planes that you are transcending which will help you work in the Records. At the end of this chapter I'm going to guide you through the planes to the Akashic Records on the Quantum Field, but first, let's get deep into these planes!

THE PHYSICAL PLANE

The Physical Plane is the plane that you live in now. You probably understand this plane pretty well, so it only needs a brief explanation.

The Physical Plane is the densest and slowest vibration out of all the planes. Here, time and space make themselves known. You've come here on Earth, and, if you're reading this book, you've most likely have been here before. Even if you feel you've had a lifetime living on some other planet, you are still part of the Earth plane. You have the genetic material and energy of the Earth because you have the same DNA as your ancestors that are part of the Earth.

My suggestion to you is don't try to deny your earthliness. When you deny that you have Earthly DNA, then you deny the work that needs to happen for you. You need to work through every aspect of yourself including anything locked in your DNA to ascend through the linear Karma and be able to master the Physical, Emotional and Mental planes.

Once you start working in the Akashic Records on the Quantum Field, you won't feel so disconnected from the Earth, and you will start to appreciate what it is and what it has to offer. The Physical Plane is a Divine gift! In my opinion, it is one of the most Divine gifts available to any sentient being.

On the Physical Plane, you can experience the creation of a physical object from the ethers. On the other planes, we can create, but we are creating ether from the ether. Here we create physical from the ether, how much fun is that?

THE EMOTIONAL PLANE

The Emotional Plane connects to the emotions and thoughts that are sent out from human beings on the Physical Plane. Everyone interacts with the Emotional Plane often since it has the closest vibration to the Physical Plane.

The Emotional Plane is a reflection of the Physical Plane. It is dualistic like the Physical Plane. We interact with the countless dimensions connected to the Emotional Plane. For ease of explanation, visualize these planes as split into two groups of corresponding frequencies: lower and higher. As you move through the planes, the vibration of each plane changes frequency. It becomes less connected to the denseness of the Physical Plane. Therefore the vibration becomes less dense as you move through the planes.

Remember that technically the plane is spiral energy and within each plane is the other plane. It is not linear. However there is a *difference in the energy and vibrations* of these planes, and the difference is between denser and less dense energy. Think of it this way: one kind of vibration is closer to the Physical Plane, and the other vibration is at a different frequency as you move through the planes.

Your interaction with the Emotional Plane happens not just through your individual experience but through the collective experience of everyone on the Physical Plane. In other words, it is a collective consciousness experience that accumulates on the Emotional Plane, and the emotional energy becomes stronger since so many people are constantly feeding it.

Lower Vibrational Aspect of the Emotional Plane

The thought forms and emotional energies from the Earth Plane accumulate on this plane, making it a reflection of both the Earth and the Physical Plane, so it holds both the positive and negative thoughts, feelings and energies that we all collectively project outward. There is a very strong emotional hold here which is why the energy of our emotions have so much power over us. You and so many other people have difficulty moving past their emotions. When you have difficulty moving past your emotions, or you emotionally react, you have not mastered the emotional energy connected to the duality of the Physical Plane.

Higher Vibrational Aspect of the Emotional Plane

Since we incarnate on the Physical Plane, that means all of us are still mastering the Physical, *Emotional and Mental planes and the Physical, Emotional and Mental bodies.* Many tend to reincarnate on the Earth plane because they are working through some of the emotional energies they didn't deal with on the Physical Plane.

Archetypes are represented on this plane because of the emotional vibration archetypes have. An archetype is a concept that represents the ideal, perfect example of a thing, or a universal symbol, or character. Carl Jung, the creator of the concept, felt there are many different archetypes, but he highlighted twelve main types or ways of being that he felt embody the human psyche. Some examples of archetypes are the hero, the queen, the lover, the sage, the innocent, or the rebel. Since all people are so connected to this plane, we all emotionally connect to the archetypes. The thoughts and emotions connected to the archetypes, or the collective unconscious, are collected here. We can tap into that collective consciousness to transcend it.

You are always connecting and interacting with this plane through your emotions which, in turn, bring the emotional experiences back to you. If you are an emotional vibrational match to a certain experience, this plane helps create that experience in your life.

Again, all the planes interact with each other, and you create on all the planes! Once you realize this, you can start using the Akashic Records to help you move past the difficulties and attachments you have on these planes so that you can transcend.

Like the Physical Plane, the Emotional Plane is also a plane where there can be many illusions.

MENTAL PLANE

Most people who incarnate on Earth are mastering the Mental Plane, as well as the Emotional and Physical Planes. The material matter on the Mental Plane is less dense and vibrates at a higher frequency than on the Physical and Emotional planes. On the Mental Plane, there are fewer particles (matter) and more light energy (waves) as opposed to the Physical Plane where we experience more matter which is why it is dense energy.

Everything created on the Physical Plane *has* to be created first on the Mental Plane as a thought or idea. Since creation on the Physical Plane starts in the Mental Plane, it then begins to gain denseness on the Emotional Plane as it connects to the emotions which are a perfect vibrational match. Once the vibrational match from the Mental and Emotional planes come together, the energy becomes a denser vibration which then becomes a physical possibility on the Physical Plane.

I am explaining exactly how the law of attraction works within the cosmology of creation. You have thoughts about what you desire, and the vibrational match comes back to you. Let's say you keep thinking about changing your job, so those thoughts go into the Mental Plane as a vibrational frequency. The feelings and thoughts about hating your job vibrate out and connects to the Mental and Emotional planes. These vibrations start to become more and more powerful as you think the thoughts and feel the emotions.

You are energetically communicating with the Emotional and Mental Planes, so they start to bring experiences to you on the Physical Plane that match your thoughts and feelings. These may be all sorts of things including new job opportunities, possibilities of losing your job, or an accident or illness that leaves you without a job.

Even if the thoughts and feelings seem like they are just in your head we live in a spiral energy system where every energy is interacting with the others. When you have a thought or an experience, it has already started on the Mental Plane then moves into the Emotional Plane and you experience it on the Physical Plane. It's like a piece of computer code; you make a change in the code, and it spirals out and makes changes in so many areas of the whole software program.

Your interactions with the world around you include interacting with the planes! You think your thoughts and feelings only affect you, but they are creating your reality and all of your experiences. Too many believe that if they have positive thoughts, they should create a perfect life, but most of your thoughts are subconscious so you're consciously *unaware* of them. Positive thinking is only part of the equation. The other part is your subconscious feelings, thoughts, and beliefs.

All creation on the Emotional and Physical planes comes through the Mental Plane. As a human being, you are *feeding all energy vibrations through thoughts and feelings into all three*, Mental, Emotional and Physical planes. These planes are also interacting with you whether you know it or not. You are constantly communicating with these planes through your emotions and your thoughts, which, in turn, are communicating back to you. The planes communicate with you through thoughts, feelings, opportunities, and experiences, like when you meet new people, get a job, have an argument and every other experience. *Every single thing* that you've seen, felt or experienced had to come through all of the planes to manifest in your life.

Since you are in constant communication with all the planes, the energy flow is symbiotic. You send it out and receive it back. It's a perfect dance of energy. To see how it all works, take Sharon, for example. Sharon divorced five years ago, and she is trying to create a new romantic relationship. She talks about dating and finding her perfect soul mate.

If it were just her conscious thoughts that would help her to create an amazing partner, then he would have shown up years ago! In reality, Sharon is constantly berating the men in her life: her father, her boss, and her sister's husband. She sees them all as backstabbing and unreliable. She is very angry and bitter toward men, and she's not aware of that at all. She tells me that she has the perfect man in mind for herself, and is manifesting him to come into her life.

What happens? Sharon doesn't know how to create change in her life, so she starts creating things along the lines of the same old pattern. Sharon's last two boyfriends have been disloyal and emotionally unavailable. At first, she falls in love quickly, but these men start to do things she perceives as disrespectful which makes her angry. These men are not showing up from just the words she thinks or says like, "I attract an amazing life partner." The men she attracts are coming as a result of the words she says as well as the thoughts and feelings about *other* men. These feelings do not match her goal, but the Universe is sending her a match for the emotions she is putting out.

All of this starts on the Mental Plane. Sharon sends the subconscious negative vibrations and thoughts about men into the Mental Plane, and the Mental Plane finds a vibrational match in a few different men. The Emotional Plane starts to connect to the emotional vibration Sharon is expressing, and the Mental and Emotional Plane start to work together to bring her what she desires which are unconscious thoughts, feelings and actions, not what she said she was manifesting.

Sharon now meets Jordan who is a perfect vibrational match, and he has been sending a signal out that he wants a woman who will despise him, so he doesn't have to commit to her. Here is your match made in heaven, Sharon.

Sharon and Jordan meet by some strange coincidence (you know, the Universe brought them together) and they fall deeply in love. One year later their love affair has ended with anger and bitterness.

There are also positive stories of manifestation. My son, Connor, worked very hard in High School because his dream was to go to an Ivy League or similar school. On paper he was a good match but getting into those schools are not guaranteed. We toured many of the schools, and he narrowed down to his top 2-3 schools, but he had a number one that he thought was his dream school.

He applied early to a few schools and got deferred to his number one school. He applied to a few more schools, but he still wanted to get into his number one school.

In March of his Senior year in High School, he finally found out that he didn't get into his number one school, but he did get into a few other schools. His heart broke, and it showed.

Within two days of getting the news about his first choice, my happy boy was back. He told me that, although he was disappointed that he didn't get into his number one school, he was excited to be going to a school in Boston that had a great Business program.

Connor said that he gave himself one day to be upset and then he would be happy to be going to the other school. He knew that he was going to get everything he desired and more especially if he put positive energy into it.

During his first semester at the school, he felt at home there, volunteered, and received amazing grades, and made lasting friendships. He knew that the school he chose was the best one for him, even if it wasn't his number one school. He also knew that going into the semester with positive thoughts and feelings would help all of the best experiences unfold.

The thoughts and feelings you put out into the Mental and Emotional planes will bring the perfect vibrational match for you, even if your ego wants something different.

When you understand the planes, you will understand where all your creation begins. Accessing the right plane will be how you will have more success working and healing at the highest level of the Akashic Records.

The Akashic Records can help you transform all the thoughts and feelings you're placing into the Emotional and Mental planes to be a match for creating a life more in alignment with what you truly desire. I am going over every detail, from understanding what you are doing in the Akashic Records, why you are doing it to how you can work with the Records. Once you start to experience the huge shifts, you will be amazed and joyous!

LOWER VIBRATIONAL ASPECT OF THE MENTAL PLANE

In the lower Mental Plane, you start to discover living light. The vibration of light feels alive and very creative. It will move and shift to help you create a vibrational match to the energy you are communicating to the Mental Plane.

On this plane, there aren't any distinguishing features like landscape, but you do create what you experience and see here. It's the energy you put behind your thought forms that start to create your experience on Earth. These thought forms can be created and stick around the plane, or you can be sensitive to the thought forms other people have created and energized here.

There is an accumulation of thought forms on this plane, and some of those thought forms could be around for hundreds of thousands of Earth years. Thought forms that are a vibrational match clump together like a cloud and this is what many on the Earth plane connect to when creating their reality.

For example, the thought forms related to the concept of, "there is not enough," or of lack. They can begin to accumulate, and you may connect to and add to that thought cloud when you are thinking about not having enough money or time. As more and more people connect and feed the same thoughts, the metamorphic field of those thoughts accumulates and become stronger. When you connect and work on this plane in this situation, then, you start to create matter or form in your physical life because the thoughts about not enough, and the energy vibration of lack, start to create a vibrational match of lack on this plane.

As human beings, we can become obsessed and start thinking in one direction, or in absolutes. When we are so connected to the absolute thoughts, we connect to a form cloud or metamorphic field on the Mental Plane.

An acquaintance I've known for many years believes that anyone who does not believe in Christ as their savior is going to hell. There are no acceptations for this rule for her. She is absolute in her thinking. She is connecting to the Mental Plane form of absolute sin, or something similar to that. How things work is a more subjective reality, but it is black and white in her mind. Her creation is being fed not just by her beliefs, but by *anyone else who has the same belief.* In other words, she, and everyone who has the same beliefs are feeding the energy cloud of similar thought forms. They are giving energy and receiving energy back from the same vibrational cloud energy.

On the Mental Plane, there isn't a right or wrong belief or energy; it's all just vibration. There's still some duality, but it's less dense than the absolute energy on the Emotional and Physical planes.

LOWER VIBRATIONAL ASPECT OF THE MENTAL AKASHIC RECORDS

On the Lower Mental Plane, there is a manifestation of the Akashic Records which connects to human existence. It is a reliable source for your personal Records. If you work in these Records, you will not connect to the full range of information that you could access through working in the Records on the Quantum Level. The Records on the Quantum Field will provide the deeper transformation available to you. Here you can find past life information and past connections, but you won't be able to see the full understanding of your part in every situation or access the complete awareness of your true self. Here you can become fully immersed in the Records and see a 360° view and from every angle. In other words, you know every thought, experience, feeling, and connection for everyone who was affected by the event. In the following chapters, you'll learn more about the kind of things that are missing from these Records but are accessible through the Records on the Quantum Field.

HIGHER VIBRATIONAL ASPECT OF THE MENTAL PLANE

As you move into the higher vibration of the Mental Plane, the energy becomes formless since the consciousness aspect of existence governs this Higher Mental Plane. Matter particles are not part of this plane, although the thought of the energy of matter will start to take form here. There is no dense material or particles of matter on the Mental Higher Aspect, just pure consciousness.

The Higher Mental Plane is free from all illusion so nothing can be hidden or avoided. If you've worked through the other planes, and come to work more from this plane, you become less restricted by the thoughts around you. You are less likely to get caught up in subjective reality, and you will begin to see the bigger picture. You will be less caught up in the worldly energies and become more compassionate and loving, even with those you should hate by Earthly standards.

In the Higher Mental Plane the energy connects information from all the Universes, or the Cosmos, that influence the human experience and the Earth Plane.

Connected to the Higher Aspect of the Mental Plane is the Quantum Field. Once you do the meditation below a few times, you will easily pass these lower planes and shift right into the Oneness vibration of the Quantum Field.

QUANTUM FIELD

The Quantum Field is the level of pure creation. It's the next vibration after the Higher Mental Plane, although the two are closely related. Once you experience the meditation below you will start to comprehend the vastness of the Quantum Field. Once you reach the Akashic Records on the Quantum Field, you will be able to transcend and heal all the issues connected to the planes below this space.

If someone you loved needed to go to a doctor for a heart condition, you wouldn't send him or her to a general practitioner. The GP wouldn't be at the level to heal your family member or friend because of the doctors training. You would want them to go to a specialist who would see the whole problem.

You want to go to the energy frequency of the Quantum Field since this is the level of creation. It has a higher vibration than the lower planes, and that vibration is available to help you transcend your lower vibrational patterns. When you work at this level, you can comprehend the whole picture including the role you play in it, and master the

Physical, Emotional and Mental planes and bodies because the higher vibration of the Quantum Field causes instant transformation.

The Quantum Field is one with all the fields connected to it, including the Earth. As you learn to work in and create in the Quantum Field, these possibilities and connections for growth become more available to you. You begin to have profound experiences more often. Life will feel less limited and more expansive. You will also start to experience a more intense Bliss feeling, which feels like a download of light energy. Now you are truly allowing yourself to experience the Quantum Field and become open to transforming so you can embrace more of your true potential.

Akashic Records on the Quantum Field

Many who connect to this plane see the world and their experience as multidimensional. Once you start going into the Akashic Records on the Quantum Field regularly to unwind your past Karma, you will start to experience your reality from this plane, which will connect to the Quantum Field and the realm of possibilities.

Since this is the source of your higher self and higher knowledge, when you start connecting to this plane, you will start to anchor more of your higher consciousness into your body and become a multidimensional being in the flesh. You'll bring that accelerated evolution into your Physical body and your life.

In the Quantum Field, there is pure consciousness. Here is where the purest energy of creation resides. The Akashic Records on this plane provides you with a more expanded view than the Records on the lower planes.

Within the Physical, Emotional and Lower Mental planes, matter (particles) is the primary or main creative energy. Since matter is the primary energy and it is so dense, you can become stuck in the illusion, and people connect more with the matter than the expansive energy of all that is.

The Akashic Records on the Quantum Field is where you start to connect and understand how creation happens, and where you will fully comprehend how Karma relates to your experience. You can let go of some of the denser vibrations of, the lower planes here because you can access higher vibrations. These higher vibrations open you up to a light and clear feeling.

The Akashic Records on the Quantum Field is pure consciousness and is sometimes called Oneness. The Records are a collective consciousness and are the highest, most reliable information associated with our planet. The Akashic Records found here contain the most loving, living Records available to you.

These Records hold not just the information from our planet but the whole cosmos as well. Everything around us, including the most subtle energy, resides here. All the Records of everything that happened in all the planes below this plane become warehoused here. When you read the Records on the Quantum Field, it allows you to experience the *fullest* scope of the event or situation. You are not just seeing the human experience, but all the mental and emotional Karma connected to it plus so much possibility for what could be. Here you will experience vast healing, transcendence, and creation!

You'll learn more about Karma in Chapters Seven and Eight, but, remember; Karma is just the emotional and mental junk that we store in our energy bodies. It's not a punishment. Karma is a way for us to understand that what we do and say matters to our consciousness, and to the consciousness of other sentient beings. Unwind the Karma and allow yourself to embrace higher vibrations.

This plane is where you can find all the detailed information about how creation starts and the vibrational possibility of it becoming matter. In other words, creation starts here! When you start working in the Akashic Records in the Quantum Field (Oneness Field), you are going to the source of healing and creation. Akashic Records on the Quantum Field is the ideal place to connect: If you can access *all* of this, then why would you want to get your information and healing from anywhere else?

All ancient knowledge is within these Akashic Records. The cosmic creative process is open for you to explore and learn about it here. Think about all the things you wish you could create in your life, including joy, a fulfilling career, and good relationships. You can connect to this plane and utilize the creative energy from the source of creation here to make changes in your life possible.

Any spiritual concepts or esoteric knowledge you would like to tap into are available in the Akashic Records in the Quantum Field. When you read your Akashic Records (or anyone else's) from this perspective, you can see how the creation of the situation or Karma started and how to unwind and heal the past so you can create something new.

SPIRAL ENERGY OF THE PLANES

All the planes exist within each other like a spiral or a toroidal field. In Chapter Three, you'll learn more about the toroidal field, but it is important for you to understand how all the planes interact with each other and yourself.

The planes of existence are not linear; they are spiral energy. The spiral concept helps you visualize how all the planes are constantly interacting with us through a vibrational frequency. That frequency comes through the toroidal field, or through a flow that works spirally.

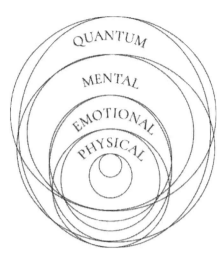

There is a reason this drawing isn't perfect. It is supposed to help you visualize, at least a little, how the planes interact and coexist. The planes are a living spiral that is in constant motion. Each plane exists within and part of the other. You can't have plane 1, the Physical Plane, without plane 3, the Mental Plane. These planes are constantly interacting and moving which is the nature of the planes.

Being on this planet, we are trained to see things with a beginning and an ending point, like a fence that delineates between two properties. In the more subtle energy of all the planes, the concept of a solid boundary can't exist, it's impossible to have that type of energy limitation.

There is more and more scientific research coming out all the time about the energy around humans, and the things around us. New research shows how our thoughts influence the smallest energies of particles and waves.

Quantum Physicists have shown that we are all interacting with the objects around us, even if there is a physical border between our body and the object. The same laws are true for the planes. They are made up of energy, as well. The planes are cooperating, and interacting with us as well as interacting with the other planes.

When I connect with my intuition and intuitively see people's Physical, Emotional and Mental bodies, I don't see those bodies as separate. The collection of all the bodies is a constant movement and flow of energy. These bodies are always changing colors and have different hues.

These bodies change size and shape depending on what is going on with the person.

To me, observing someone's energy looks like a dance of flowy movement, like a kaleidoscope. If someone is depressed, their energy feels and looks muddy, and the colors look dull, and the size and shape of their energy is unique, depending on what they are feeling, as well as depending on the person.

The planes have the same type of energy movement, and the energy within the planes is constantly fluctuating and changing. It is a movement that resembles moving in a multilayered spiral, and the energy of the planes interact within each plane, and the planes interact with your energy bodies.

Since the planes are always interacting with each other, they are in constant flow, and this flow is circulatory. As you connect with the Akashic Records on the Quantum Field, you are also interacting with all the other planes. That is why this healing is so deep. You are going to the highest Records of all, and transforming on not just that level, but *all* the other energy levels tied into it.

MASTERING THE PLANES

Now that you understand the correlation between your energy bodies and the planes of existence let's talk about why this information is so important. In Chapters Seven and Eight, you'll go deeper into Karma, but for now, it's important for you to get the gist of the reasons why mastering the planes and your energy bodies will help you in transmuting your Karma and in your Ascension Process.

What does it mean to master the planes? It means that you can master the energy of your Emotional, Mental and Physical bodies. You are going to experience reverberating energy from your Karma until you transcend it, so you want to do that transcending and start to master each plane. When you have mastered and transcended the planes, you will be less likely to get caught up in the drama of the Earthly plane, or the issues with your physical body. You will see beyond the drama of those around you, and no longer be triggered by any situation or event. That includes political, spiritual, and family drama. When someone posts something on social media that makes you angry, scared, frustrated or emotionally or mentally disturbed, this is an example of you getting caught up in the drama. You'll be less attached as you master the planes.

Since you live on the Physical Plane, you will still have some feelings. As you master your Physical, Emotional, and Mental bodies you move through the feelings that come up more quickly and easily and you become less triggered by these situations. Although these situations seem important at the moment when you are working with your Karma, and people may feel righteous about having strong feelings and emotions about it, the truth is that it is all an illusion. It's an illusion, so it's up to you to master these planes and bodies to transcend the triggered emotions.

One other thing that will happen as you start to master the planes is that you will start manifesting easily and spontaneously. Your life will flow easier, and you will start to feel more blissful.

Now that you understand the Planes, and how you benefit from mastering them and connecting to the Quantum Field, you will learn how to connect to the highest level of the Akashic Records.

Before You Begin the Meditation

There are several meditations in this book which will build on the previous meditation, so when you get to Chapter Nine, you will be able to access the Akashic Records on the Quantum Field easily and do some major healing there. Since this is the first meditation, it's an important building block to help you expand your awareness into the Akashic Records on the Quantum Field. Be open to allowing yourself to relax into the meditation.

Your intention is to expand your consciousness past the Earth and the Physical, Emotional and Mental planes so you may connect to the Akashic Records on the Quantum Field. Expanding past these planes helps you move past the duality into the Oneness energy, so when you're in the Records, you are open.

Would you like an mp3 recording with music? Go to the link below and download the mediation.[2]

MEDITATION-CONNECTING WITH THE AKASHIC RECORDS ON THE QUANTUM FIELD

Make sure you are in a quiet, private space. Close your eyes. Take a few deep breaths to relax your body.

Your intention is to expand your consciousness through the levels of existence into the Quantum Field where the Akashic Records reside. You will know you are in the Quantum Field when you are in the space of nothingness, and you feel love and connection. There is nowhere to go. The Akashic Records are right here. All you need to do is surrender, feel your consciousness expanding and know that the intention is to connect to the Quantum Field in the Akashic Records.

Bring your awareness to your heart. Feel your consciousness expand. Feel the energy around your body. Your intention is to expand your consciousness past the Earth and the Physical, Emotional and Mental planes so you may connect to the Akashic Records on the Quantum Field.

---

[2] https://melissafeick.com/rar-meditations/

As you feel your awareness expand past your body, you become aware of the Earth and feel yourself becoming one with the Earth. Expand your consciousness into the Universe, past the stars and planets and become one with the Universe. Feel your consciousness expand past the Universe and the Physical Plane. Now your intention is to move past the Emotional and Mental planes into the Quantum Field of the Akashic Records. Your consciousness already knows what to do, surrender into the process and allow. Keep expanding into the Emotional Plane and then past it. Expand into the Mental Plane and become one with the Mental Plane.

Feel your consciousness expand into the Akashic Records in the Quantum Field. Be present with the energy. Notice that right now there isn't anything to see or do. It is pure energy. Open your heart and feel the Oneness and unconditional Love.

Take a few deep breaths. Take another deep breath and breathe into your toes. Feel your body and become aware of your body. Bring your awareness to your feet and then to your heart. Open your eyes.

You shouldn't need to ground since you are just expanding your consciousness, connecting with the Earth and not leaving your body, but if you do need to ground drink some water and walk around outside.

CHAPTER 3

TOROIDAL FIELD

By this point, you may have noticed that the spiral is a major theme used throughout this book. Although I talk about the energy being a spiral, it is a Toroidal Field. Understanding the Toroidal Field, or spiral will support your comprehension of the energy dynamics of the levels of existence, of your energy bodies and the Akashic Records.

The Toroidal Field is also known as the Torus. It is an energy system found everywhere in nature from the smallest atom to entire galaxies. The recurring pattern of the Torus is an activated energy shaped like a vortex which expands out from the top of the cone, wraps around the outside of the spiral, and then returns into the bottom of the vortex. The Torus has a natural movement, and its fundamental system can be either complex or simplistic. It is like a five-dimensional spiral. The Torus is what you would call a fractal geometric shape, and every atom in the universe is a spiral or fractal. Arthur Young is a scientist and philosopher who has written and spoken about the Torus. He explains that the Toroidal Field is a dynamic energy pattern that can sustain itself and is actually, "...made out of the same substance as its surroundings like a tornado, a smoke ring in the air or a whirlpool in water."

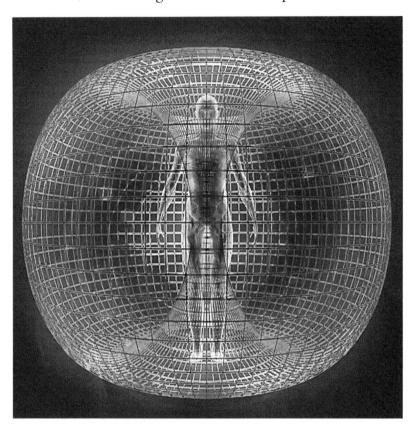

The HeartMath® Institute[3] has researched the Toroidal system around the human body and what they discovered is that the Heart is the strongest energy source in your body. Many people would like to think that the strongest energy centers around their head or brain, but nope! Science shows it's the heart. This institute found that there is a Toroidal flow of energy that flows from your heart upward and outward around your body and then back to the bottom of the heart.

---

[3] https://www.heartmath.org/research/

It's no mistake that the Torus is found in all of nature, as this energy flow depicts how we interact, energetically, with the world around us. The way the universe converses with us is through energy, using a language of energy and geometric symbols. As an intuitive, I have seen how this energy interacts with people, but the fascinating understanding that this model is how we connect to the higher planes and dimensions. Since we are multidimensional beings, we can connect with many other energy systems beyond the Earth through the movement of the Toroidal Field.

The Toroidal flow is the way the Universe has an energetic conversation with you and how you can communicate back to the Universe. The Universe, or Quantum Field, is consistently bringing you what you are asking for with your energy whether you are asking consciously or unconsciously. So if you emanate anger and frustration from your heart into the field, you receive that frustration energy back to you. When you emanate higher frequency feelings like Love, Joy, Oneness, and Gratitude from your heart, then the Quantum Field flows the same joyful vibration back to you.

This is very important to understand that the frequency of your heart and where you place your thoughts or intention is what the Universe hears, and exactly how the Universe or Quantum Field speaks back to you! Chapter One we discussed how you are always creating and the energy that emanates from your heart either helps you create an amazing life, or creates a sucky life. I want you to understand that this not so you can feel bad about yourself for your negative thoughts or feelings, but to, instead, empower you to create more of an awareness. The awareness of the energetic play between you and the world of energy around you can assist you to make powerful decisions working in the Akashic Records and your life.

The electromagnetic Toroidal Field around you is in constant motion, and it's always interacting with the Earth's electromagnetic field and the Quantum Field. In Chapter One, you learned about illusion and creating your reality. Your Toroidal Field is also energetically interacting with other people around you, which means you are picking up subtle cues and vibrations which, in turn, help you to understand your relationship with those people. These interacting energies are creating your reality and co-creating reality with those around you. You may not realize that you are also giving subtle signals from your Toroidal Field to other people, just like you do with the Universe. So if you'd like to create more loving relationships, be sure to expand your awareness here, as well.

Toroidal Flow

The Toroidal Field involves constant energy movement, i.e., Toroidal flow. Since the Torus is a fundamental form of energy occurring naturally, it is always expanding and returning to its source. As it moves outward, it collects like energy (energy that is aligned), and it connects back to the origin. For example, if you are feeling pure love and gratitude, the Toroidal energy of love flows outward and connects to the Quantum Field which then collects opportunities and experiences that make up the vibration of pure love and gratitude and then brings all of that goodness in the flow back to you. What people call the Law of Attraction or the Law of Magnetism is the Toroidal flow. The Toroidal flow of another person is what either attracts you to them or repels you from them. It is the entire energetic vibration-matching process.

Think of it as a beautiful energy dance of two or more Toroidal Fields in which one expands outward, interacting with all the fields around it until it bumps into another field that resonates in frequency, and then it brings that frequency home to visit you.

The Quantum Field

It is the Akashic Records within the Quantum Field that allows you to heal and create or to manifest what you desire. In working with the Akashic Records, you want to reach the Quantum Field because this not only holds the information from the Universe as it is now, but the Quantum Field also contains everything that could be possible. In this book, you are learning how to reach the Akashic Records on the Quantum Field through the use of the Toroidal Field, and your consciousness.

Take note: The key to your creative abilities and your deep healing is the awareness that you are not a victim of your circumstances.

You are powerful. You can create what you want and desire from the energy system called the Quantum Field. I want to empower you with the understanding that once you spend some time in the Records and connect to the Quantum Field, you will feel on purpose and be able to create what you desire.

While in the Records on the Quantum Field, it will be fast and easy to change and rearrange all past events. You will be able to change the roots to your current and future experience and manifest different things. As you heal and rearrange the past events, either past lives or events from earlier in this lifetime, you recreate your past. When you recreate and reconfigure your past, you then recreate your future. What is possible for you is likely to change as new possibilities rapidly open to you.

When you hold onto your past, you live the same life you have always lived. You know the past and, likely, if you are reading this book, there are things you don't want to live again! If you hold onto all of that past anger, hurt, guilt, and fear you've felt in the past, then you reflect that energy into the Quantum Field, and it then returns that same energy back to you. It's important to take your power back by utilizing the Akashic Records to recalibrate your past and create a new future.

If you feel like you have lived a life of pain and sorrow, then the reality is that you are living in the past. You don't want to keep reliving those difficult experiences over and over—that's the opportunity this book presents to you: to finally be free of that same old crap.

The Akashic Records hold all information from the past and your *possible* future. You always have the power to choose what that future has in store for you, no matter what you've felt so far in your life. The Akashic Records knows the truth about your soul's fullest potential and wants to help you connect to everything you need to feel that truth. Through the Records, you receive healing and the awareness to reach your fullest potential.

This field is made up of pure potential, so when you are in the Records, you are healing on a deep level, and you are helping your DNA calibrate to a new potential for yourself.

Your Toroidal Field and the Quantum Field

Your Toroidal Field and the Quantum Field are constantly interacting with each other. They are communicating through the energy of feelings, like love and joy. If you close down the possibility of receiving love, the Quantum Field can't envelop you in that energy.

I have mentored, done intuitive readings and facilitated healings on thousands of people and the aspect that I hear from spirit is that too many of us are unable to receive. We shut down the energy of receiving because of our feelings of unworthiness, fear or countless other feelings that consume us.

If your energy is not open to receiving from the Quantum Field and the Akashic Records, the love and guidance you've been asking for will be unable to connect with you. It is time for you to surrender and let go.

MEDITATION EXERCISE

At the end of the next chapter, there will be a meditation. It will include connecting to your Toroidal Field to interact with the Quantum Field.

Chapter 4

Heightened State
of Awareness

We already established that the Torus is an electromagnetic field of energy and that HeartMath® Institute has shown that the heart is the strongest electromagnetic field in the body. Since the Toroidal Field is constantly interacting with the heart and the other electromagnetic fields around us, our reality is constantly interacting with and created from these energy fields.

When you feel love stir inside your heart, the electromagnetic field vibrates the frequency of love around you which activates a Toroidal Field. Your Toroidal Field of love stretches outward into the larger field around you and connects to the energy and reality of love in a greater sense.

The heart is significant to humans in that it is the first internal organ created in a fetus. The heart has its own brain to regulate its movement which indicates that it has its own intelligence. The heart is responsible for sending signals to the brain so that the brain will release essential hormones and electrical impulses into the body. When your heart is open and your head quiet, you will become more peaceful, open, cooperative and less aggressive. You will also be more connected to Truth.

It is the heart space and the energy from the heart that helps you connect to the concept of Oneness. If you disconnect from your heart, then you are disconnected from your intuition, your connection with your higher guidance, and the Quantum Field.

Your emotions, when they come through your heart, are constantly interacting with other people, the Quantum Field, and the world. You can create a cohesive energy flow in your body through appreciation, compassion, gratitude, and love, which creates a ripple effect through your energy bodies, your life and the energy around you.

The head and the heart have different vibrations. As you go about your day, the head creates thought forms that can have a profound impact on your life. Some of the thought forms around your head can create confusion which keeps you disconnected from your heart. There is a difference between thought forms that originate from the ego, thought forms from the heart and thoughts from your Higher Consciousness. How do you know which is which? Many of my students and clients ask these questions because they want to know which thoughts are supporting them. What you need to know is that Higher Conscious thoughts are like an instant download of information and wisdom and they have a calm, peaceful feeling to them. In contrast, ego thoughts, which can accumulate around the head, are more like rolling thoughts that switch directions and intensity. These thoughts from the ego voice can activate your old wounds and create havoc with your feelings which will then activate an imbalance of energy in your bodies and chakras. The experience of engaging with ego thoughts is not smooth at all—this is how you can know that you have lost your focus on the connection with your heart.

Gregg Braden and HeartMath® have done studies on the brain and heart connection and have found that the two can either be out of sync or in coherence. To be in coherence means to form a whole or to integrate. When the higher consciousness and heart are in coherence, there is a peaceful feeling. My guidance from the Akashic Records is to integrate all your energy, so you are in complete coherence which is part of the ascension process.

This ideal state of coherence involves the integration of all your energy chakras. It is best to do that before you connect with the Akashic Records. When your thoughts are quiet, and your chakras are aligned while connecting to the Akashic Records on the Quantum Field, you become more connected to the Divine Source. Not only does this feel peaceful and help you in your personal ascension process, but this also creates a heightened state of awareness. This awareness then helps you access the Akashic Records even more clearly, which benefits the level of accuracy and depth in your readings and the healings you receive.

For now, focus on coherence as simply meaning a heightened state of awareness. You can achieve this through a simple technique that takes a few minutes and a little practice.

Coherence creates an integrated energy system. The result of a cohered, integrated energy system is balanced energy throughout every level. In this state, your heart can create on the Quantum Field without the ego getting in the way. It helps you to open up to your divinity. The ego will try to create from lower feelings, and the coherent energy helps you to be in your heart space for Divine creation, which is much more powerful.

I am going to teach you how to produce a profound clearing of the negative thought forms from your ego that have accumulated around your head. Sometimes you can pick up other people's negative thoughts; this clearing will release that as well. After this clearing meditation, you will want to activate and align all your chakras. The results of using this meditation have been very powerful to allow you to create from your Higher Consciousness, so I suggest you learn the meditation and do it often.

CLEARING THE CLUTTER IN YOUR HEAD

Are you the type of person that has trouble sitting still or quieting your mind? This meditation is very helpful and should be done before any meditation or before and during your Akashic Records readings.

Make sure to practice and master this meditation so that your work in the Akashic Records will be successful and beneficial to you and anyone you help.

Thought forms accumulate around you, feeding the monkey mind. When you take a few minutes to clear the thought forms, you will find more peace, and it quiets your mind and your life. You will also be able to create more of what you would like to experience, rather than repeating the past or creating your worries and ego.

The reason this came to me is that I would be working with people and they couldn't get out of their head or the thoughts spinning around them. I saw a dome of thoughts around their shoulder and head area, and there were so many thoughts that came from themselves and others. Intuitively, it seemed that these thought forms consumed them.

These thoughts were stuck there and had no way out until I lead my clients through a meditation. Then they were able to feel more peaceful and focused.

Your intention is to clear any mental clutter and become focused on what you need to focus on so that you stay centered on love and spirit. The meditations for clearing the clutter and activating your chakras are below. You may also like the mp3 downloadable mediation on my website.[4]

---

[4] https://melissafeick.com/rar-meditations/

Meditation to Clear the Clutter in Your Head

Close your eyes and focus on your breath. Feel it slowing down.

Bring your awareness to your heart chakra. Feel your breath as you breathe through the heart chakra area. Feel your heart expand with every intake of breath and let a calm wash over you on the exhale.

Bring your awareness to the area around your shoulders and head. Notice all the chaos or chaotic thoughts, energy or feelings that accumulate there.

Your intention is to release all the thoughts that are stuck here. Release any thoughts from yourself or the ones you have picked up from others. See all the thoughts lift off into the light that is all around you. You are releasing their hold on you and releasing your attachment to them.

Once you sense the quietness of having all the thoughts release, bring your awareness to the back of your head where a girl would have a high ponytail or in the back of your third eye chakra. Notice the silence there.

Now bring your awareness to your heart. Stay there for a minute and sense the opening of your heart. Here you will continue the second half of the meditation in which you will activate and align your chakras.

Do this often, especially before meditation or Akashic Records Readings.

Activating and Aligning Your Chakras

Once you complete the above meditation, you will want to activate and align your chakras. In order to be in full coherence you will need to clear your thought forms and activate and align your chakras. When you experience full coherence of your chakras, connect to your heart and feel it open.

Your intention for the meditation below is to activate each chakra 1-8. Once the chakras are activated, your intention is for them to align. This activation and alignment will happen organically but keep your focus and intention on the meditation.

Once you complete the activations and alignment, your Toroidal Field will activate around you. This activation will open your energy up to a higher vibration and help you connect with the Akashic Records.

MEDITATION TO ACTIVATE AND ALIGN CHAKRAS

Your intention is that you are going to activate and align each chakra starting with the root chakra. Close your eyes, take a few breaths and imagine your body relaxing.

Bring your awareness to your base or root chakra. When you feel into that chakra, say, "Activate" (to yourself, not out loud) and feel your root energetically activate.

Now bring your awareness to your second chakra, the sacral chakra. When you feel into that chakra say, "Activate" (to yourself) and feel your sacral chakra energetically activate. Imagine the root chakra aligns with your sacral chakra. These chakras are now in perfect alignment and activated.

Now bring your awareness to your third chakra, the solar plexus. When you feel into that chakra say, "Activate" (to yourself) and feel your solar plexus energetically activate. Imagine the root and sacral chakras align with your solar plexus. They are all now in perfect alignment.

Now bring your awareness to your fourth chakra, the heart. When you feel into that chakra say, "Activate" (to yourself) and feel your heart energetically activate. Imagine the root, sacral, and solar plexus chakras align with your heart. They are all now in perfect alignment and activated.

Now bring your awareness to your fifth chakra, the throat chakra. When you feel into that chakra say, "Activate" (to yourself) and feel your throat energetically activate. Imagine the root, sacral, solar plexus and heart align with your throat. Now your root, sacral, solar plexus, heart and throat chakras are in perfect alignment.

Now bring your awareness to your sixth chakra, the third eye chakra. When you feel into that chakra say, "Activate" (to yourself) and feel your third eye energetically activate. Imagine the root, sacral, solar plexus, heart and throat align with your third eye. Now your root, sacral, solar plexus, heart, throat and third eye chakras are in perfect alignment and fully activated.

Now bring your awareness to your seventh chakra, the crown chakra. When you feel into that chakra say, "Activate" (to yourself) and feel your crown energetically activate. Imagine the root, sacral, solar plexus, heart, throat and third eye align with your crown. Now your root, sacral, solar plexus, heart, throat, third eye and crown chakras are in perfect alignment.

Now bring your awareness to your eighth chakra. When you feel into that chakra say, "Activate" (to yourself) and feel your eighth chakra energetically activate. Imagine the root, sacral, solar plexus, heart, throat, third eye and crown chakra align with your eighth chakra. Now your root, sacral, solar plexus, heart, throat, third eye, crown and eighth chakras are in perfect alignment and fully activated.

Now feel the energy open and activate around your whole body like the Toroidal Field. The movement of this activation completes the energy system.

Stay present without thoughts, be the observer of awareness and the energy of the Toroidal Field. Now open your eyes and come back to the here and now.

CHAPTER 5

AKASHIC RECORDS

Once you start accessing the Records, you will begin to understand the magnitude of information available to you. I want you to start to access and utilize the Akashic Records which will truly change your life!

Whether it is your romantic life, business, or money karma, you will find that your relationships and life will transform through the information you will discover through the Records. Not to mention this will deepen your connection to Spirit, which, as you will see, is one of the most important things to help you be happy in your life.

THE REAL REASON YOU ARE HERE

When I access the Akashic Records for one of my clients, I first ask, "What's the most significant piece of information this person needs?". This way, I can see where they need to focus. I usually ask them to come to the session with a list of questions prepared, but sometimes the Akashic Records shares some crucial information.

As I write this to you today, there's an important piece of information that wants to make its way to you. Do you know why you are here on the planet? Have you ever wondered?

The real reason why you are here is to transcend your own *Karma.* Yes, this is why you are here!

According to the Records, it is important that you know that, *yes,* you can transcend your Karma.

You are not and never can be a victim of life's circumstances.

Let me ask you this: Have bad things happened to you? Have you had disappointments? If you feel like you must have bad karma, or feel like you've spent ages trying to figure out a solution to be happy, know that you *have* found that answer. You can stop waiting to be happy. You can radically transform your life today and be happy right now.

So how can you do this? You are holding the answer in your hands: You can transcend your Karma by using the Akashic Records.

The Akashic Records can give you a view of your life that is different from anything else. Think of the Records as a TV station that you can interact with and it has every signal available to all times in history.

What can you see there? This TV station can give you the most important information about you and your history. When you do this, it will show you a synopsis of your lifetimes and the specific patterns of your Karma that will help you see the bigger picture of your existence.

Since the TV station is interactive, it will help you heal and transcend the issues that come through and help *you have a clear awareness.* You'll see not only the plot of the stories that you have lived through but also the impact you have on all the characters, the depth of your transformation and the ability to see why you had that experience. You'll understand why those events were necessary or you'll learn from it in an entirely new way.

When you work in the Akashic Records, you are literally "in" the Records, or "inside" the energy. Even if you do not do anything, like ask a question, or see or hear something, it's transformational to even be in the energy of the Akashic Records. It is *limitless energy*. You will feel freer as you connect with it. I am so excited for you to dive in and grow as you learn to use the spiritual technique of accessing the Akashic Records.

WHAT ARE THE AKASHIC RECORDS?

The Akashic Records that you will be accessing contain all the recordings of everything that has happened or will happen within our Universe. All knowledge and information are available within them, including everyone's lifetimes, relationships and experiences. There is not only information about you, but there is also the vast totality of information about every other soul that has ever incarnated within the Universe. The Records hold the knowledge of all civilizations, planets, and universes that exist.

The Records are a *living archive* of every single conscious experience in the Universe, including every thought, emotion, action, or situation, as well as the cycles of stars and planets. The living Akashic Record created for each event is an energy imprint or *a living vibration* that has its own energetic consciousness. That consciousness collects and stores *all* vibrational information. Think of the collection of Records as not only a vibrational representation of every experience you've had but of every single sentient being in our Universe!

This collection of information is like a hologram: each piece taken of a hologram replicates the whole, rather than being merely a slice of a greater whole.

Akasha is the element of spirit. The Akashic Records is the living Akasha. The Akashic Records connects to the Divine, so don't worry, its very nature is not to judge you or prove what you did was wrong. This living energy is neutral so that it has an increased ability to show you the truth about all aspects of your existence. *This Divine assemblage of vibrations is there to show you exactly where you can improve your life and what things it would be best for you to release.* In the Akashic Records, the deepest healings happen when you use the energy or information available to see and to transcend your old patterns so that you can be more aware of how to live from your soul self.

You have free will, meaning that what you do in the Records and how you utilize the information is up to you. These Records can assist you in seeing the truth, getting deep into your experiences as a soul and, yes, this will help you in your life now. Remember, it is all your choice, but the Records want to help you see your old patterns and let you transcend them.

Akashic is a Sanskrit word meaning 'radiate' or 'shine,' 'space' or 'ether.' These Records hold the energy vibration or imprint of every event, thought, and emotion, and how it relates to *all* those involved. (You may be surprised how far the web of impact around an event can go and how many people may be involved or affected by every event held in the Records. Everyone and everything in the Universe is interconnected.)

What can you do with these Records? You can refer to your Akashic Records to find out about your Divine purpose, what your Karmic patterns are, or how to transcend relationship issues. You'll see which past lives are impacting your life now, how family Karma is playing out, how to overcome your troubles with money and so much more! When you go into your Records and ask about any situation, you usually are shown a combination of the above scenarios. You may ask a question about a current situation and then be shown information like how it relates to your past lives, how to deal with the situation, what patterns it connects to and how it affects your Karma. In Chapters Seven and Eight, you will go much deeper into Karma and the real healing benefits of working with the Records.

The Records have different levels and frequencies which are available for you to work in and explore. In this book, I'm teaching you to connect primarily to the level that gives you the opportunity to shift Karma and to experience deep healings. Since the Records on the Quantum Field are a living, conscious vibration, you have the opportunity to use the Akashic Records to heal and transcend old Karma every time you're there! You may not know this even if you have learned about the Records elsewhere. The living and transformational quality are available to you, and I want you to access the full transformational potential. *Know that the Records are living vibrations and trust that your connection to them will assist you in reaching your highest good.*

The Records are a living energy which is why they shift and change. For example, if you have had a pattern of betrayal throughout many lifetimes and you transcend it this lifetime, then your Records reflect that evolution. Once you transcend a major Karmic influence, you no longer need that vibration anymore, so the Records will shift to reflect how you overcame betrayal and will begin to vibrate at a different frequency. *The Records assist you in shifting the old stories of betrayal into a new vibration so that they become the stories of transcendence.* Do you see how powerful this is? No matter what you've experienced, you are not stuck. It is not doom and gloom if you're stuck in an old pattern. You can literally rewrite the story that is in the Records. The power of the Records can assist you in your healing, transformation, and ascension.

Another reason that the highest vibration of the Records can shift the vibration of your life experience and more is that *they exist beyond space and time.* In this space beyond space and time, you no longer have a past or future, there is only *the eternal now.* This eternal now will reflect any healings instantaneously and become the living record of the *eternal now* of your soul as you change and grow here on the planet.

Although the Records are in the eternal now, you still have an awareness of past, present, and future, so that you may use the Akashic Records to connect with your possible futures or future experiences. For instance, if you were to marry a particular person, what would your future look like? Note that the Records will only give you a few possible situations since you always have free will, and you haven't created your future yet. But seeing these possibilities can help you become aware of what may happen and then determine what would be a good choice for you so that you can transcend your Karma. The Records will show you the possibilities of each choice you can make should you need to decide something important.

The Akashic Records connected to the Earth plane, which is a record of everything in *our* Universe, helps those of us on Earth to transcend. There are also other Records which hold all the information for *other universes.* Because the focus of this book is radical transformation here on Earth, the processes here are just for the Records associated with this Universe. You have incarnated on this Earth plane to transcend your Karmic patterns, and the Records can help you to do just that.

THE AKASHIC RECORDS AND OUR UNIVERSE

The Records archive the entire history of everything a soul experiences since creation and all that soul's interactions. That includes the entire history of every thought, action, feeling, and deed. The Records store your Karma, your family's Karma, the Karma of a nation, and so on.

The Akashic Records are special because they not only contain information, but they also have a transformational vibration. The Akashic Records are always influencing us from afar with this living frequency. In Chapter Three, you learned that the Toroidal flow is the way the Universe has an energetic conversation with you and how you can communicate back to the Universe all you receive and manifest. Since your Toroidal electromagnetic field is constantly interacting with the field around you, it draws Karma, people and situations to you, including what you need to heal, from the information and vibrations held in the Akashic Records. When you are in the Akashic Records on the Quantum Field, you have the opportunity to heal on so many levels. This profound healing can transform your life.

If you are looking for answers to your soul or life purpose or soul connections, you will find that the Records holds all the wisdom. It holds the wisdom of not only the Soul Purpose but how to express the soul's essence in this lifetime and what is holding you back from allowing that expression.

The Akashic Records not only hold all the experiences and events, but it also has all the mystical knowledge and esoteric teachings. These teachings in the living archives are accessible to those in alignment with the knowledge. In other words, those who would use the knowledge for the good of all have access. If you use the knowledge for negative purposes, you will be unable to access those Records. All this mystical, esoteric knowledge encoded in the Akashic ether is available for you to access if you are a vibrational match.

The only exception to that rule is that if you already have access to the knowledge in your Records, you can use the knowledge any way you choose. If you want to use the wisdom of how to lead people from your Records to start a cult that worships you, you can gain the wisdom from your personal Akashic Records.

As you read in Chapter Two, the Akashic Records reside on a few different planes of existence. Anyone can access the Akashic Records on the lower planes, and the Records on the Quantum Field are also available to anyone. In Chapter Three, I explained that it's wise for you to work and access the Records on the level of the Quantum Field because this not only holds the information from the Universe as it is now, but the Quantum Field also contains everything that could be possible. So make sure you follow the meditations and directions to utilize the Records on the Quantum Field.

HEALING WITHIN THE AKASHIC RECORDS

The Records are a living imprint of all information and energies. These Records can be shifted and changed as you release old ties, emotions, patterns, and Karma, which is the ultimate reason to work in the Records: for healing, raising your vibration, and ascension. When you are in the Records, you are changing the energy and shifting so much on so many levels. The energies stored here are living vibrations, so anything in the Records can be unwound, or disentangled, and recreated. You are not destined to live the same experience over and over again. You can transform your past in the Akashic Records.

While you are in the Records, you can experience your past actions through a Divine understanding of your Karmic patterns. The Records will show you lifetimes of the same pattern and how it's affecting your life now. With this information, you can ask the Records to help you see the pattern on a mental, physical and emotional level. The next step is to unwind the Karma to transform and heal yourself or your clients. This healing can be very deep or superficial. The depth of healing depends on the person and if they are ready to let go of the pattern. The Akashic Records will only be able to heal to the depth of your willingness.

The Records are part of the Universal Consciousness or Collective Consciousness which we also tap into for our intuitive answers. What you want to do is go beyond the Collective Consciousness and go into the Records and receive the bigger picture or a 360-degree view. It's always up to you what you choose to do with the information.

When you are connecting to the Records on the Quantum Field, you can heal on so many levels. While in the Records, take the initiative to unwind your past and create your future. You can see any event and perceive it from all perspectives. You can feel how your actions affect others and how you felt. *It's important to see all angles because to unwind Karma and the old energies you have to take personal responsibility for your part in the situation and forgive yourself and all involved.*

You are using the Records while in the physical body to overcome the Karma and other energetic patterns. Healing in the Akashic Records is so simple, and the best part is that the process is fast, effective and enlightening. The more you work in the Records, the more you gain back your power from reincarnation and Karma. When you begin to utilize the Akashic Records to access the deep healing available there, you begin to understand your Karmic patterns which help you to ascend and master your Physical, Emotional and Mental bodies. You will begin to discern the world and your actions as more of the observer and create more consciously.

You're also able to transcend your emotional ties to major events that happened in the world. If you are emotionally triggered by 9-11 or by pornography or any situation or event, *you become energetically entangled* to that event or situation. When you experience an energetic entanglement to an event, you are Karmically connected, and any Karma around the event affects you and your ability to raise your vibration and ascend. You can be Karmically entangled with political parties, advocate groups, races, areas, events, people, places, nations, etc.

We will go into greater detail about becoming Karmically entangled in situations when we talk about Karma in Chapters Seven and Eight. For now, look at the Akashic Records like a video you can edit and rearrange to create the result you desire. This editing in the Records happens through the unwinding and healing process.

Accessing Another Person's Akashic Records

To access someone else's Records, you must have their permission. You can't go into your boyfriend's Records to see what's going on. You can go into your own Records and see what's going on between you and how your relationship with your boyfriend affects you.

The Akashic Records are a sacred tool for personal transformation. It's impossible to use the Records to heal another without their consent or to change others' Karma.

Reading & Healings within the Akashic Records

Once you connect to the Records, you will make the intention of what you want to accomplish in the Records. It's easiest to start with a specific event in this life that has an emotional charge for you. You are not supposed to be experiencing the event. Your intention is to understand all aspects of the event or relationship and to experience deep healing.

You want to see the whole pattern from the beginning which means you may be shown other lifetimes with this person or other lifetimes where you experienced this pattern. Be open to the pattern within your family and how this pattern formed with other people in your life.

One reading I did was for a man who was in his late 50's. He wanted to know about his difficult relationship with his daughter. He said that she wouldn't visit him and only contacted him when she wanted something. As I connected to the Records, I became instantly aware of all the lifetimes with his daughter. His Records allowed me to see right away how his relationship with his daughter was the same relationship that he had with his mother. Resentment and manipulation was the Karmic pattern. With his permission, I did some healing within the Records and helped him to release the cellular memories by unwinding some family Karma associated with this pattern.

The healing went as deep as the client was able to go. He said that he understood the information I shared from the Records, but he was only grasping a small portion of the Karma. He couldn't appreciate the full picture because he was having difficulty seeing his personal responsibility in the relationships. It was easier to blame his mother and daughter and to see *them* as the cause of his suffering. He was unable to completely heal this pattern because there was still some other Karma he needed to work through but we did get to some of it.

The greatest benefit of doing healings in the Akashic Records is that once the healing is *complete,* your Records change. Even if you have a multi-layered Karmic pattern, you are still healing and transmuting the Records. These are living Records which change and transform as you heal and transcend your Karmic patterns.

Steps of a Basic Healing

For you to get an understanding of working in the Akashic Records, I added this basic outline for healing in the Records. You will get an overview now, and we will go into much more detail in Chapter Nine, Working in the Akashic Records, where you will be able to immerse yourself in the healing energy of the Records. The next few chapters will create important groundwork, so you get the deepest healing available in the Records.

1. Know that any situation or Karmic pattern is just an experience in the human body and the cellular memory will shift once you let go of the need to hold onto the past. Your impression of the situation will start to feel like a distant memory once you have released all Karma. That is when you know you have transcended the Karma.

2. Get deep into the personal responsibility, which means to take responsibility for your actions. Taking responsibility is a major key to the healing process.

3. Unwind, transcend and surrender all feelings and energy around it.

4. Forgive yourself and all involved. Have compassion for yourself and others.

5. Ask the Records how to see it differently.

6. Know that it is not real and that it's safe for you to let it go and unwind it from your cellular memory. (The reason you heal within the cellular memory is that the imprint of the Records is in the cells of your body.)

7. Ask to experience your greatest potential and allow that feeling to envelop you.

The detailed process of working in the Records is in Chapter Nine, Working in the Akashic Records.

CHAPTER 6

LIVING A MORE CONSCIOUS LIFE

While in the Akashic Records, you are accessing the aspects of your life or lifetimes which you came to Earth to transcend and heal. This quantum change allows the amazing soul of who you truly are to shine through. When you are in the Records, you can choose to take a look at your patterns, or you may choose to heal and overcome them.

The deepest and most profound healing will happen when you are *very honest with yourself* and take responsibility for all your actions, past, present, and future. To take responsibility, you want to look at every aspect of the situation and ask to see all the Karmic patterns and Karmic ties. Be open and willing to change any beliefs or values you are attached to. You will ask lots of questions while you are working in the Records. How is this pattern like my family patterns? How did I feel? Where did this Karmic pattern or Karmic tie originate? What can I learn? What else do I need to know to experience the deepest healing?

It's all about taking personal responsibility for every area of your life, relationships and actions. When you do this, you are no longer the victim and take your power back. Taking responsibility is not about blame. It's about recognizing the what and why of your life, as well as your physical, emotional and mental patterns. This full awareness helps you live a more conscious life.

As you work in the Records, you will start seeing patterns in your life and any past lives that connect to them. If you want to overcome Karma and let go of the lower aspects of yourself when you are in the Records, then you unwind the energy and take responsibility for your actions. Taking responsibility for your actions assists you in overcoming the Karma because the Karma can't be there if you no longer are emotionally connected or upset. It would be like the Karma never existed at all because when you are in the Akashic Records on the Quantum Field there is only pure potential. Karma can dissipate, or it will recreate the energy. You are in the energy of pure creation and potential.

Karma is the emotional imprint of energy that is stuck in your DNA and within your soul. Once the energy is unwound (transformed and healed) and you let go of the emotional charge, you have space in your energy to become the Divine essence of Unconditional Love, Inner Peace, and Oneness.

If you still feel upset or you think the situation is someone else's fault, you still hold Karma around that situation and are Karmically entangled with that person. You will read more about this in Chapter Eight and how it can occur at the level of a family, group or nation.

A good friend and I had a falling out a few years back. She was mad at me for something I did which she felt was wrong. It was not easy for me because I didn't know why she was so mad and why she just stopped talking to me. Finally, she explained her perception of what happened.

I was able to understand how she thought it was a betrayal. I was upset, and I also felt guilty. The feelings I had were mine and had nothing to do with her, so I had to take personal responsibility for all of my feelings. She did not "make me" feel guilty. When you blame another for your feelings, then you are in victim energy, and you are not taking responsibility for your actions. I realized that betrayal was the theme of this situation since I felt betrayed and she also felt betrayed.

Betrayal is one of the Karmic patterns that all humans have to deal with at one point or another. I knew that this was important and I knew I would have to do this several ways and several times to heal and unwind the majority of the Karma around this event.

I decided to go into the Records and look at all aspects of the situation and unwind the energy and patterns around guilt, betrayal, and pain. I then went into the Records again and asked to be shown the Karmic patterns between both of us. I then looked at all the areas I didn't take responsibility for and all the other lifetimes where guilt and betrayal were themes. I have worked on this theme and everything the Akashic Records has brought forward. I asked which lifetimes were connected and the origin of the pattern of betrayal. It is important to know that there is no need for blame or victimization. I also asked the Records to show me any other Karmic ties I had to betrayal, guilt, and pain in my family or anywhere else. When you are in the Records, you want to get all the energy connected to any situation even if it doesn't seem connected; this is about taking back your power and healing your past wounds and Karma.

I wanted to be no longer Karmically entangled with this person, and I found myself able to feel complete forgiveness for myself and her. If I became emotionally charged in any way, I knew I still had work to do, and I would go into the Akashic Records again and ask questions and unwind and heal anything else that came up. If I didn't take personal responsibility, I would never have been able to let go of the Karmic entanglement and heal the Karmic issue.

Once you have transcended the Karma, then you have completed the cycle. You are no longer Karmically entangled even if the other person has an emotional tie to you or the situation. It is up to the other person to do their own healing work.

You can only clear the emotions, Karma, and Karmic ties if you take responsibility for all aspects of the situation. When you take responsibility, you can transcend the Karmic energy quickly.

Sally, my client, had a sister, Cathy, who was very upset with her because *she said* Sally told her that she abused their mother. Sally had no idea what was happening. Very calmly, Sally asked Cathy what she meant. Cathy proceeded to tell her that they were talking about how their mother does not want to go to the hospital or to have any medical intervention if she got sick. At that time, Sally said "it would be abusive if mom broke her leg and we did not take her to a hospital". They both understood why their mother would feel that way and the conversation didn't go any further.

A while later Cathy called Sally and accused her of saying *she was abusive to their mother*. Sally said that was not how she saw the conversation at all and told her that she was sorry and that she didn't mean to upset her. Sally explained that she would never intentionally say something so horrible. Sally has done some deep inner work with me and was able to take full responsibility. She told Cathy that she understood that this upset her and knows that she is responsible for how she makes her feel. It's not about being right or wrong. In the Akashic Records, there is no right or wrong, just energy connections. In these situations, if you hold onto the energy, you become energetically entangled with the other person. Sally took the time to unwind anything that is still in the Records and take responsibility for her part, so she wasn't entangled with her sister.

You're the Creator of your Life and Experiences

You are creating your future through your action *or* your inaction. In the Records, the best transformation happens when you heal and unwind your past, which allows you to create a better life for yourself. You are the creator of your life through your choices, including if you decide to make a choice *not* to make a decision or *not* to let go of your past. By recognizing this, you acknowledge your basic responsibility for your life.

You always have the option of becoming paralyzed by fear and doing nothing. You have a multitude of choices about what you do in response to the situations in your life. *The outcome ultimately depends on how you choose to respond.* There will always be outcomes even if you decide not to take action because making a decision is difficult. Know that when you do that, that means that you are holding onto old Karma and old Karmic entanglements because of how you are presently choosing to respond to past events. But it is never too late. The amazing part of the Records is that you can undo ALL events. It is the beauty of working in the Akashic Records.

Sometimes reviewing information in the Records can bring up a lot of feelings. If you are emotionally charged by an event while working in the Akashic Records, you can ask to see the event as an observer. When you do this, you are allowing the Records to show you how to see the situation in an unbiased manner. Remember, the Records hold the energy of your Karma and patterns, but they do not judge whether your Karma and patterns are good or bad. The Karma is just what it is, and if you let go and become present with your emotions and release the emotional charge, then there are more opportunities for growth and healing. Many times when you transcend or let go of something within the Akashic Records, it changes the energy of the situation and your relationship with that person, place or nation in your physical life.

The Akashic Records are available to help you understand not only that you can undo past events and connect with your higher consciousness, but it may also help you understand why it's important to live a more conscious life. The more you connect to the Records, the more you will see how the world works and that all the things you thought were so important no longer seem important. Once you realize this, you start taking an active role in your life. You are more likely to recognize when you are emotionally triggered and when it is time to go into the Records for more healing work.

As you work with the Records, you start to make decisions more consciously. You make your choices based on the higher understanding and how you interact with the Quantum Field and the Akashic Records. By consciously choosing how you respond to events, both in action and thought, you are taking responsibility for your experiences in your life.

I know that taking responsibility for your actions, working in the Akashic Records on the Quantum Field, and being conscious will help you feel more empowered in your life. You can no longer see the world as making things happen to you. As you work in the Records, you can see, instead, how you can create the world you desire and a more magical life!

You will become more confident in difficult situations and be less emotional. You will be less likely to give your power away to the moment or your emotions. You are starting to take charge of your life. That is so empowering!

HAPPINESS AND POWER

If you live in your mental chatter of worry or the emotional turmoil of sadness or anger, then you do not have any room to be happy. The Akashic Records are all about allowing you to experience your true Divine essence without the limitations of the human mind or emotions.

When you are too connected to the story of any situation, you give your power to the situation which makes you unhappy. When you take responsibility, you take your power back which creates joy and happiness within.

As you work in the Records, you'll begin seeing your humanness from the perspective of your soul, or higher self, which heightens your self-worth and your ability to find peace and joy in every situation.

AKASHIC RECORDS AND CLAIMING YOUR POWER

The key to feeling powerful is how you respond to the information that is being presented to you while you are in the Records. Once you see how easy it is to overcome the situations, you will stop giving your power away to new situations that come up. You will start to become more aware of your boundaries and stop giving your power away to your inner victim.

The victim energy has sucked the energy out of you for lifetimes. I know this because it is frightfully common in our society today. Don't buy into it! The Records will show you something else entirely. Once you take your power back, you will have a bunch of energy to create the life you desire. You become the creator of your destiny instead of the victim to your destiny.

While you are in the Records, ask to see yourself honestly and to see the way other people perceive you. Ask lots of questions to get the full understanding of higher consciousness and ask how you can create the life you desire! Remember, this is not so you can judge yourself harshly. Looking at yourself honestly helps you feel more empowered and more in love with life.

CHAPTER 7

TRANSCENDING KARMA

Karma is a key element to the evolving soul, especially in such dense energy as *Earth*. Karma is the Law of Attraction, and your vibration is a reflection of your Karma. You are connected with all the people in your life because you are Karmically entangled. You attract these people in your life to become completely aware and present with your Karmic entanglement so you can transcend it.

A significant aspect of healing Karma is to be open to your actions and reactions to the events in your life. **To experience deep healing, you will need to take personal responsibility for yourself.** The spiritual master teachers always stress personal development to their students. It's through personal development that we transcend our Karma.

The best way to know if you are working on your Karma is if you are working on yourself. It is **not about achieving perfection; it's about cultivating self-realization, which means looking at yourself and your actions honestly and without judgment.** We spend lifetimes working through the same Karmic patterns because most people are not self-aware. Be different. Decide on one area of your life that you want to start transforming and go into the Records for guidance. When you make major inner and external transformations, you know you are working on your Karma.

When you begin to recognize the Earth from the perspective of a higher consciousness, you will see through the illusion, and your Karma *naturally starts transforming*. You came to Earth to transform and master the Karma which accumulates in your Physical, Emotional and Mental bodies.

I have heard many spiritual people insist that there isn't any Karma. They don't believe God is handing out Karmic punishment for misdoings. I agree, Karma isn't about punishment, but if they are denying Karma, they are missing the amazing opportunity to transform and transcend their Karma. You don't need to believe in Karma for it to affect your life. It is part of your experience here. The Law of Karma is what attracted all the things in your life, like your new job or your best friend.

I also have heard people say how they worry that Karma will never end and that every second you are creating more Karma. This fear holds you in the illusion that it is impossible to overcome your past and your past Karma. That is such an unfortunate belief. Karma isn't a tally sheet. It is an **opportunity** for growth and transformation.

You can only hold onto Karma if you hold onto the lower emotional and mental pain that the Karma has caused. Most Karma comes in patterns, and once you realize we are all working on the same patterns you no longer need the Karma attached to those patterns, you can transcend them.

When you give your power away to ideas like these, you are not taking responsibility for your actions and for who you are. You are not a victim of your Karma. You have the ability and the tools, through the Akashic Records, to transmute any Karma, past, present, and future. It's time for you to take back your Karma from the Karmic hamster wheel and transcend into your higher state or full potential. Once you transcend and master the Physical, Emotional and Mental planes and energy bodies, you also transcend your Karma, which is what the Ascended Masters have already done.

TRANSCENDING YOUR KARMIC PATTERNS

The Akashic Records are a *living* energy that is in constant movement and transition, just like your energy field, or aura. Your energy field is a reflection of your current state of mental, physical and emotional health. Your aura's energy and colors are constantly moving. It dances and swirls around you the way a river rapid flows around rocks. The colors all intersect and move within each other. It is not really about the color of your aura which changes with circumstances and moods; it's about the clarity and brightness of the energy around you.

The Akashic Records are moving around and dancing an energy dance. Since it is a living energy, it can be shifted and changed. So once you transcend your Karma, then that old Karma is expunged from the Records. As you dissolve more and more of your Karmic patterns, the easier it is to access the positive soul Karma and positive soul qualities. Karma works through the Law of Attraction. Wouldn't it be nice to have your soul qualities more present in your life and to have a greater connection to your higher consciousness? You have that potential as you work within the Records.

Your Karmic patterns use the Law of Attraction to guide you to master the Physical, Emotional and Mental levels and bodies. We are all stuck in the wheel of Karma which is the reason we incarnate on Earth over and over again. Being caught in the wheel of Karma means you are *getting caught in the illusion or the false reality of the self* that you believe is who you really are. That self would be considered the ego identity. So many see the self as a name, a job, and a family. It has stories of hurt and anger, but this is only a reflection of the truth of who you are. The ego's identity is the illusionary self and can be changed and transformed by doing the work in the Akashic Records. When you go into the Records, you start to understand the limitations of the egoic identity, or those things the ego believes to be true. The ego itself is a part of the illusion. What's the truth of who you are, really? The truth of who you are is not the ego; it is the whole Divine self. When you clear the old patterns in the Akashic Records, you start to dissolve the ego identity and become the higher consciousness identity of All That You Are. In Chapter Eleven, I will explain more about the ego and reality.

Most souls reincarnate because they are still working on Emotional Karma, Mental Karma or Physical Karma. Do not assume that just because someone has physical limitations that the only thing they are working on is on the level of the Physical body or Karma. It is also possible, for example, that they could have wanted to transcend the Mental body and they chose to do it through physical limitations. People are different, which is why the Records will give you specific information for each person you work with during Akashic Records readings. You can transcend it all.

No matter what type of Karma you are working on, when you start working in the Akashic Records, you will notice that the process is the same. Your intention in the Records is to transcend the old Karmic patterns.

The wheel of Karma is more like a spiral. As you move up, you may come back a little, but the movement is always outward toward expansion and Oneness. The reason you are moving in this spiral is that, habitually, you will keep seeing yourself as the ego-self and you will get drawn back into the illusion. You reincarnated into this lifetime because you were still holding onto the past story of your emotions, anger, and resentment. You didn't transcend the illusion in the last life, so you needed to come here again to work through the same patterns. You have the gift of transcendence available to you through the Akashic Records right now, so I suggest you use the Records fully. You are moving toward the Oneness and raising your vibration so you can become your true self while in a physical body.

ILLUSION

Transcending your Karma means working through the illusions that are present in your life and your past experiences. These illusions hold you back from your true potential and keep you stuck in repeating patterns. When you release the illusion, you can better achieve your dreams in your love life, your career and more.

Illusion and Karma are closely connected, as you transcend your Karma you transcend the illusion and vice versa.

Illusion is a very abstract concept because of the world you live in is dualistic. Since you live in a world of duality, it is easier to explain and understand things in absolute terms, such as light and dark, old and new, up and down. This duality causes your ego to see your surroundings in a limited way. All your senses have limits. As your ego uses those senses to understand the world, it is easy to believe that what the senses tell you is the only reality. The truth is that your perception of reality connects you to your consciousness and any change in your conscious awareness modifies your reality. It is possible to see beyond this limited ego vision of the world and start to see new things as you expand your consciousness.

Have you heard the term Oneness or that we are all One? If we have a world of duality, how can we all be One? I understand that these two concepts can be contradictory. The illusion is that on the lower planes we see and experience everything as separate, even when a mother carries a baby inside their womb the baby is thought to be separate from her mother. Spiritual leaders, mystics, and ancient texts explain how the separation is an illusion. We are all One, and the concept of separateness is an illusion on the Earth plane. Once you connect to the highest level of the Akashic Records, you will begin to see and experience the Oneness.

Oneness comes from the Divine. For years I was told about Oneness, and I thought I understood it and believed it, but it wasn't until I had the experience of Oneness that I could embrace the depth of it. I want you to grasp that our world holds separateness as truth; but hasn't that separateness created war, violence, anger, hurt, and destroyed our planet? That is the illusion that we are separate from each other, the planet, the world and from other nations. In reality, we are all the energy of the Divine Oneness, but we lost that understanding when we moved into this realm. When you came to the Earth plane, you started to feel separate from Divine Love, and you became caught up in the illusion of the linear, dualistic energy of the lower planes which keeps you in the wheel of Karma.

To reach this place of Oneness which is all around you and available all the time, you need to be aware and conscious of what your ego does every day to create the illusion of separateness. All of your limitations contribute to an understanding of what reality is. When you view the world through these limitations, you see reality as understood through your ego; this is your *ego reality*. This ego reality also includes or connects you to your perceptions, feelings, moods, and the environment, including the environments of the past, that make you feel stuck in life and stuck in Karma. Since this reality is how we navigate our world, the ego believes the Earth is the only reality, and it gets fed this false belief by experiencing more and more of the Earth's riches. The ego chases desires and grasps at anything to feel better; it is the ultimate consumer. When you feel separate, you look to the world to fulfill your craving.

The truth is that there is nothing outside of yourself that will completely fulfill your need for connection and love. The ego wants you to buy into this illusion, that something 'out there' will make you feel loved, satisfied or happy within. Buddhists believe we are looking toward the illusion to become whole and feel connected. They call it grasping: you are grasping at your desires but you never really get what you want. It's hard to get what you want when you look outside yourself for love and connection. Those positive feelings connect you to higher states of consciousness, and you can only really become those higher states when you transcend the illusion. Now, instead of wanting something in the external world to fulfill you, by transcending the illusion and Karma, you attract all sorts of amazing things and experiences because your energy is a higher state of consciousness.

The human mind is limited. Since it usually only senses what's around you, it's difficult to grasp the concept that there is something more than a piece of cake or a lover which will make you happy. You are conditioned, from an early age, to believe that what you see, feel and experience is real.

It is important to recognize when the world around you is only reflecting back the projection of your mind and the minds of others which is different than the Law of Attraction. The Law of Attraction attracts things to you that match your vibration and Karmic patterns. You see the world around you through a limited kind of lens, which causes you to see more illusions. It's a distorted version of what's going on since you are so attached to what your subconscious reflects back to you. Your mind and senses create your personal reality when you are living in limited consciousness. In Chapter Eleven there is more detail about the nature of reality, and how the brain is responsible for how you perceive that reality. Remember that the mind and senses limit your consciousness from seeing that we are not separate, or that the reality is that we are all One.

Synesthesia is when people naturally combine senses. They can smell, feel, hear or taste colors. Can you taste colors? If you can't do that, think of this as an example of how you are living in a limited world. There are more ways to perceive the world around you, but you are missing something.

There is an existence of something outside your human senses and projections. As you start meditating and accessing the Akashic Records, you can begin to perceive beyond the limitations, and your consciousness becomes more connected to the Divine. Expanding to connect to the Divine unlocks your extrasensory perceptions like clairvoyance.

Human senses have a limited capacity to reflect back to you the truth. Imagine walking into a kitchen and smelling the aroma of cookies, but then as you look around you don't see any cookies anywhere. You think there should be cookies since your sense of smell is sure there are cookies. But what about other possibilities? What if the cookie smell was a candle? Did your senses deceive you?

Did you see the blue sky yesterday? So you believe the sky is actually blue, right? Or is the blue sky an illusion? In actuality, the sky is not blue at all, and we only know that because science has "proved" that to us.

Even time and space, which seem so real, present illusions. On Earth, we experience existence as a linear concept; it seems like time passes minute by minute, and one thing happens after another, but this is part of the illusion of time and space. Believe it or not, physicists have now scientifically proven how small units of matter can occupy the same time and space in a vacuum. It sounds crazy, but it's true! I've even witnessed things appearing and disappearing, which has helped me comprehend the illusionary world. I have had my sunglasses disappear from my car and reappear under an acquaintance's car seat even though it seemed impossible because I have never been in their car. I have had $5, and 10 dollar bills literally land at my feet with no one around me. These are just a few stories about the illusion and how to think outside the box and transcend it!

We live in the illusion where things like the car we drive seem real, but what does "real" mean? What does "reality" mean? Are things only real if we can see or touch them? What about the WiFi in your house? You can't touch the frequency of WiFi or radio waves, but you know that they are real. Certain limitations and illusions that you grew up with are the assumptions you make about what is real and what is not. It's not until you transcend the illusion and the Karmic patterns that you will start to comprehend reality beyond the illusion.

Hinduism goes into detail about the concept of Maya, or illusion. Leaders in this tradition consider our world to be illusory. They conceive of the world of existential reality as being the illusion, void of the pure consciousness of creation. The religions of the Far East have emphasized meditation; it's through meditation and Divine contemplation that the spiritual practitioners will begin to see through the illusion and begin to understand reality.

Your experiences in your world are just temporary reflections of your perceptions, thoughts, and feelings. Scientists have done studies to find out how humans filter the sensory perceptions of our world. They have found that there is so much information bombarding our senses, but humans only retain a small amount of it consciously.

The dream state is a great example of limited perceptions. When you are dreaming, you may think that what you are dreaming is real. You wake up thinking that the item you had in your hand is still there but it's not, it was only in your dreams.

So is your dream real or are the experiences you have when you are awake real? Both are projections from your subconscious and can change as your beliefs or feelings change. Have you ever been so in love with someone that you perceived them as loving and kind but later your perception of them changed? How could you perceive them so differently in just a few years? Both perceptions are projections of your mind. You are creating the experience from a deep desire or a subconscious program.

The illusion is all about perception and how you perceive the world around you. Different people see the world in different ways. The person who has money in the bank sees financial opportunities everywhere. Meanwhile, even if they live in the same town, the person in poverty sees only the lack of financial opportunities. Nothing is permanent about how you see the world. It is all based on how you currently project your fears and desires outward. Remember that you do this because you hope for love and joy within. There are easier ways to feel love! All you have to do is connect to the Records, your true potential, and Oneness.

Death is another example of an illusion. You think that when someone dies, they are gone forever—but time and time again people have passed on only to come back through medical intervention. Many times those survivors share memories of crossing over and meeting their spouse, parents or other loved ones on the other side. These common stories explain how no one really dies; they just move to a different vibration.

LIVING IN THE WORLD OF ILLUSION

When you live in the world of illusion, you become stuck in Karmic patterns. Transformation is possible when you see through the illusion of the mundane you and begin to switch your focus to look towards the Divine you. The mundane illusion is that you are a person who has certain roles in life. These roles could include that you are a parent, who drives a certain car, who wants to travel, who has certain likes or dislikes, etc. The reality is that when you die, you will no longer be the role you play in life or own a car, etc. What is the real you? Is how you appear to others based on the perceptions of this world? Or is it the spirit or vibration you will become when you cross over? You hold that frequency now already. It is easy to be so focused on the mundane way of looking at things that you deceive yourself into believing that this Earthly version of reality is so real. The truth is that the mundane, or ego reality, is all a projection of your thoughts outward so that you see what you want to see. If you only live in a world colored by your projections, you'll stay stuck in the illusion because you will keep gathering evidence to prove your ego reality is the only truth there is, but it is a false way to see reality.

You live in a world of drama. The drama comes in many interesting packages: the drama of family, money drama, illness, as well as the drama in your job, in society, in your country or even within the movies. All of that drama around you is an illusion because when you change your *perception* of the drama, your *experience* of the drama changes. You are here to see beyond the illusion and transcend your Karma! Everything is you, and you are everything. There is no separation. But you are choosing whether you will join in the illusion of the drama or transcend it to a higher consciousness.

The illusion is that only the form or matter of the creation around us is real. Hard cash. Results. Evidence. *But you need to know that it's not the form that is real—it's the energy that creates the form and gives the form existence that is real.* Consciousness is the *only* reality. When you alter your consciousness, your reality changes. Meditation, inner contemplation, and working in the Akashic Records are essential tools to alter your consciousness so that you can see through the illusion and connect to your highest potential.

KARMA AS OPPORTUNITY

You may be thinking that the task to shed your illusions and ego-realities is a massive undertaking. How can you move forward when there is so much to unravel? You may feel overwhelmed because you don't even know where to start.

Karma, stuck spots in your life, unhelpful emotions, and thoughts, are all opportunities for you to grow and expand to your true potential. You will find that the following chapters will teach you how to use the limitations of your life for true spiritual growth. You will not need to look far to make massive shifts in your life. When you endeavor to transcend your Karma by working in the Akashic Records, situations that may bother you right now can be huge opportunities for an increase in Joy and happiness. In this way, Karma is not a punishment or a vicious cycle at all. It's a beautiful opportunity to improve and change your life.

KARMIC ENTANGLEMENT

All Karmic connections you have, are connected to *your own Karmic patterns as a soul, so you choose the family, race, nation or group which will reflect that Karma.* We all incarnate into family units which are connected to a particular group so we can transcend our individual Karma. You are Karmically entangled until you release the past patterns you have accumulated.

You are not just entangled with other souls or people; you can be Karmically entangled to any nations and groups with which you are associated.

CHAPTER 8

RELEASE KARMIC
ENTANGLEMENTS

This next Chapter is extremely important. You may feel like a victim, unable to change your life because of your life circumstances, or the way that society is. You may feel that there are difficult things that occurred in your past and you feel suck or out of control. But what if you are actually connecting to an illusion of being stuck? And really, the truth is, that you are totally free? What if the reason you've felt so unable to move forward and change, is due to Karmic entanglement or the energetic connection to your family, a group you belong to, or the country you live in?

As you read in Chapter Seven, many people have Karma that keeps them stuck repeating old patterns, like not feeling loved or not making enough money. The Akashic Records can help you clear that Karma so you can finally break through to the truth of who you are. To do that you'll need to be aware of the way your energy becomes entangled with the energy of other people and groups. You may be surprised to realize that you are Karmically bonded not just with other souls or people in your life, but also to the nations and groups with which you associate. Karmic Entanglement is true *especially if you have an emotional charge when you think about those people or groups*. If you become upset or angry with anyone in your family, any race, nation, or group then you know that you are experiencing a Karmic entanglement. The energy that entangles you to that outside person or group perpetuates your Karmic patterns. These bonds can run very deep, and if you do not clear the energy, then it may make it much harder for you to transform things in your life. Luckily the Akashic Records can assist you in doing just that!

These Karmic bonds are what the quantum physicists call entanglement. In the energy of the world today, you can easily become entangled in the energy of others. Entanglement happens when you start to become enmeshed within a group. Being enmeshed in a group, for instance, could mean that you lose your sense of independence, and feel your existence depends on your connection with the group. I have a friend who is a strict born-again Christian, and her life became entangled with her beliefs of that religion. When you have a Karmic entanglement, your whole reality becomes the energy and belief of that group so you can also become Karmically entangled when you start to take on a belief system from another person, group, nation or race.

Karmic entanglement comes from the understanding that we are all One and interconnected. When you are entangled energetically with anyone including people or nations, your consciousness connects with them and creates an energy system. For instance, as you energetically entangle with a group of people, the accumulation of similar thought forms can make you more attached to the thoughts and beliefs of that group, and that attachment affects your Karma. I went into detail in Chapter Two about how thought forms accumulate.

Here's a situation to illustrate Karmic entanglement: You've always liked your boss, but lately a friend at work has been complaining about her. You are around this coworker all the time and, as time goes on, you start not to like your boss, and you start complaining about her, also. Now you are entangled in the energy of your coworker, your boss and possibly the organization. Because of this entanglement, you are not living from your full potential, and the negativity at work affects you more emotionally and spiritually than it needs to. When you look at your patterns and beliefs honestly, you will want to go into your Akashic Records and clear the entangled Karmic patterns.

You may feel that it's difficult to create intentional change in your life if you feel like other people are dragging you down. You can create huge changes in your life and the world by disconnecting with entanglements and rising to a higher vibration. From a high vibrational space, you'll naturally uplift other people in your life, so don't allow tribal feelings of loyalty to keep you from being who you are meant to become. If you want to be free and experience your full potential, then you want to address these entanglements so that you can become higher states of consciousness.

Although quantum physicists understanding of entanglement is a modern discovery, the ancient mystics also spoke of this entanglement when they spoke of Karma. Most physicists will tell you I have no idea what real quantum entanglement is and that is a valid point. I am not here to teach you about practical physics. I am here to help you understand how Karma becomes enmeshed in your life and how to transcend your Karma.

Karmic entanglement perpetuates the illusion of separation because we live on a dense plane in which *our physical senses support separation*. Once you start to disengage with the physical world and clear your Karma, you will see beyond the limitations of time and space.

All the Karmic entanglements you have today connect to your Karmic patterns as a soul. Before you came into a body and entered this lifetime, you chose the family, race, nation or group which reflects the Karmic patterns of your soul. You needed these experiences so you could learn or gain wholeness in a new way. You incarnated into a family unit and connected to a particular group, so that you can transcend your Karma. The soul is not looking for punishment, but you are Karmically entangled until you release the past patterns you have accumulated.

When you go into the Akashic Records, take a look at where you are Karmically entangled with any nations, races or groups and be aware of your responsibility in the situation. Basically, if you are triggered or upset about something you are responsible for your energy or reaction to it.

You will want to work through all the different types of Karma described below when you want to resolve an issue in the Akashic Records. In the upcoming Chapter Nine, I'll walk you through how to do this step by step. But first, you will want to understand all of the energetic influences that are attributing to your experiences. The possibilities for how these different types of Karma can show up for you is endless. It depends on how you choose to experience them in this lifetime.

UNDERSTANDING FAMILY KARMA

Family Karma includes all the beliefs and patterns you inherit from your family which is usually the family you share DNA with but it is also the family we have been adopted into or married into. If you are adopted you could be working through two types of family Karma, your birth parents and your adopted parents Karma.

Don't get overwhelmed by the idea of family Karma; it is a gift to be able to work through these deep issues and transcend your Karma!

Family Karma is the biggest emotional trigger for so many people; you may not want to see how much you are like your mother or father or how your family influences you. When you came into this lifetime, you chose the family you were born into so that you could work through the patterns your soul is ready to transcend and transmute. You may question why you ended up with the family you did.

If you incarnated on Earth to learn about compassion you may think that it would have been easier if you were born to a Buddhist who meditates on compassion. Most likely you wouldn't learn about compassion by meditating on it, your Karmic patterns needed you to witness pain which helped you discover compassion for yourself and others. This way you could learn about compassion directly. Instead of wishing and hoping for a different relationship with family members, why not start working through your family Karma in the Akashic Records and become open to seeing both your family and yourself in a new way.

Be honest with yourself, notice the beliefs and patterns you and your family have in common, this will help you do some deep work within the Akashic Records. When you go into the Records, you may ask about the Karmic family pattern which will help you transmute your own Karma.

You are going into the Records to get through these issues more quickly than ever before so you can finally let it all go—remember that's why you are attracted to doing this kind of inner work. You know on some level this is the key to living a happy, healthy life. The best part about unwinding the Karma in the Akashic Records is that you do not have to wait for anyone else to change: you get to change your relationships by taking personal responsibility on your own, so you have no reason to wait! You get to choose when to let things go.

When I do readings for clients many times, I see the family's Karmic patterns relating to the client's question. Once I was giving a client an

Akashic Records Reading, and she asked about her career. For this particular client, I got an intuitive message and sensed specific Karmic entanglement that she was working through by choosing this career. She was studying to be an acupuncturist and what came to me was that this was definitely outside her family's belief system. If she wanted to succeed in that field, she would need to work with this family Karma, or it could hold her back.

When she came into the reading, her Karmic pattern was that she persistently felt the need to people please and be what everyone else wanted and expected her to be. She had the pattern of sacrificing her desires and her higher guidance to be loved. Now that was paired with her awareness that she had chosen something outside of her family's expectations. She had some difficulty dealing with the depth of feeling like a disappointment to her family.

She wanted to let this go right away. So to deal with this, we needed to go into the Records and clear the Karmic patterns of having to live life according to the expectations of what others wanted her to be. We also cleared the Karmic patterns of hiding parts of her real self so people would like her.

As you do Akashic Records readings for others by following the instructions in this book, unwinding the Karma will bring new understanding to your clients. Once the person receives the reading, they can start to take a clear look at the Karmic patterns that are holding them back. It's easier for them to recognize the Karmic entanglement which gives them the ability to continue to work on their Karma after the reading has ended.

RACE KARMA & NATION KARMA

Like family Karma, every race and nation has a form of Karmic entanglement which isn't a negative or positive thing; it's just the energy we are working through on Earth. If this awareness triggers you in any way, please know that you are in charge and if you are emotionally triggered go into the Records and transcend the Karma.

Your soul has chosen what nations or races to be a part of, that means that you are using that race or national Karma to bring more experiences to help you transcend *your* Karma. You are not a victim to the race or nation you are connected to; the most exciting part is you are here to transcend the Karmic patterns you've been holding on to, and you can easily do this by working in the Records. If you are American Indian, Russian, African American, British, American or Mongolian *it is only an issue if it triggers you* or you feel like you're unable to change your life. In the Records, we are all one, and the separation of race or nation is only part of our illusion. If you feel a connection to the Karma of your race or nation, start asking questions in your Records to see how to unwind the Karma that is affecting you.

You may also be Karmically entangled to a race of people you are not genetically part of, so if you have anger or hate toward any race or nation, you will want to work on that Karmic entanglement.

Political and religious conflict would be part of this energetic Karma. For example, the Irish internal conflict which began in the1960's was both a religious and political conflict. If you were part of this war or you were emotionally upset by it, you are Karmically entangled. While in the Records you can ask what race or national patterns you are Karmically entangled with and unwind and heal it in Akashic Records. Remember, your focus in the Records is to transcend your Karma and patterns that keep you trapped in the illusion.

GROUP KARMA

Group Karma is encompassing, and you can be Karmically entangled within any group if you have an intimate connection with them. Every experience and every deed is stored within the Records' divine archives; this includes every situation or event in a particular group. If you are part of a religion, for instance, you will want to work on that group Karma. Even if your affiliation is over, you are still Karmically entangled if you have an emotional charge when you think about that group. I have many clients who have left their strict Christian backgrounds, but they still need to deal with their Karma with that church or group. It's not about the association with a group but the emotional trigger you experience. Once the emotional trigger is gone, your Karma is transcended.

Let's say you live in the United States and you are a registered Democrat. There is a certain amount of group Karma connected with any political party. Your best friend is very emotionally charged about the politics and gets angry and tends to be very vocal about the issues. She sees events happening on a broader scale as personal attacks on her. Although you have compassion for the current issues, you see through the illusion and tend to have a more balanced approach. You are probably not working through that group Karma, but your friend probably is, she's entangled in the groups Karma since she is so impassioned by it.

The best part about going into the Akashic Records and working through this type of Karma is that you may come out of it with a better ability to see the bigger picture. There is a huge difference between being emotionally charged and feeling compassion about things going on in the world and that is why Buddhists emphasize equanimity. If you have an emotional response (this includes anger) by a group, organization or association or the issues they represent, take a look in the Akashic Records and see if you can unwind and heal the Karma around that connection.

There is a very fine line when it comes to Karmic entanglement. If you believe in animal rights and you become angry and upset with a person who is a hunter you become entangled in the hunter's Karma and your own. It only affects your Karma when it affects your emotional, mental or physical bodies. But wouldn't it feel better to find modes of change while feeling more peaceful? It's all about equanimity.

Under this category of group Karma, you can also add any associations and organizations. The Freemasons and Skull & Bones from Yale are old organizations that have their Karma. Even if the Karma is ancient, you still may have a connection to things long passed. It is easy enough to go into the Records and shift the group Karma so that you are free.

In the past, I was part of a group which had the energy of exclusivity. When I started interacting with this group, I started to take on their belief systems which created a Karmic entanglement.

When I left the group, I had an emotional charge, so I had to deal with the Karmic issues within myself connected to this group. It was hard to disengage from the energy and ties I had with this group; it had become part of my identity. Once I did the deep work to transcend my Karmic entanglement in the Akashic Records, I realized how I had lost part of myself which was liberating, and I found an inner strength that helped me become a better healer and coach.

If you feel, in any way, too emotionally charged or connected to a group, go into your Records and inquire about your connection, your involvement, and your Karma. You can easily unwind your Karma entangled with the group.

All organizations you are connected or upset with are entangled within your Karma until you heal the emotional, mental or physical Karma in the Records. Transcending Karma in the Akashic Records is all about experiencing equanimity and seeing beyond the illusion of the lower planes.

KARMA AND PERSONAL RESPONSIBILITY

The key to overcoming Karma is to take full responsibility for all of your actions, this lifetime and other lifetimes. There is a huge difference between blame and responsibility. When you work with family, group, and nation Karma, you will need to remember the lesson of personal responsibility, which you read about in Chapter Seven.

The blame game is not part of working in the Akashic Records. Blaming is part of the Karmic entanglement! Once you go into the Records, you see all sides of the situation, and if you are willing, you will see the situation and the pain other's experienced because of your actions. Once you see your part in everything and you take personal responsibility, you will transcend your Karma.

When you go into the Akashic Records, take a look at where you are Karmically entangled with any nations, races or groups and be aware of your responsibility in the situation. Basically, if you are triggered or upset about something you are responsible for your energy or reaction to it, why not take the fastest way to transcend old, deep Karmic patterns.

CHAPTER 9

WORKING IN THE
AKASHIC RECORDS

I want you to get the most powerful shifts from working in the Records. To connect with the Akashic Records and get the deepest and most profound shifts, you must understand what they are, what to do while you are in the Records and why it is all important. You will learn what the Records are and how utilizing the Records will help you to live a happier, healthier life!

Now you are ready to begin accessing the Akashic Records. First, this chapter will explain the process, which is super easy, and then you can go into meditation and experience it for yourself. The meditation is at the end of this chapter. You can record the meditation so you can close your eyes and listen or buy a pre-recorded meditation on my website:

https://melissafeick.com/rar-meditations/

The Akashic Records as Spiral

I spoke earlier in Chapter Three about the spiral of the Torus and how our Universe is a spiral energy. The very fabric of your body and your DNA is made up of a spiral, or Toroidal Field. The Toroidal spiral is in constant motion and is the movement of creation. *You will utilize the movement of this spiral energy to let go of all your old patterns, beliefs, emotions and thoughts as you work in the Akashic Records.*

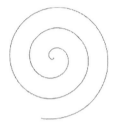

When you are healing and working in the Akashic Records, the patterns begin to release in a spiral be-cause the spiral space is also how you create your ex-periences. The cause and effect of true creation happens in the circular pattern of the spiral. This spiral of the Torus is an easy movement of energy. In Chapter Two on the Planes of Existence, I went over how the planes exist in a spiral and how every plane exists within the other.

Your past, present, and future aren't sequential. It's moving spirally. Think of the passing of time in your life as a movement of energy up and around with no end and no beginning, just consistent movement. You are used to the illusion of an ending and a beginning, but the feel-ing of time passing is really about the spinning energy of the vortex which makes you who you are. Your energy field, or aura, is spinning. Your emotions spin around you and your thoughts spin around you. The spiral is at the core of who you are. It's in your DNA. The energy of creation is the flow of the Torus; as the energy moves out and around, it goes out and back to the source. This Toroidal spiral is how all creation happens. If you are healing your past, you are creating a new present. In the Records, you are recreating your past by allowing the old patterns of pain, beliefs, feelings, and Karma to move outward in the spiral, and when it comes back around it is now a brand new vibra-tion. You literally recreate the past and the energy.

When you go into the Records, you are going to let go of your past patterns in the gentlest, easiest way. You are unwinding the past by unwinding the feelings, unwinding the beliefs and patterns, and unwinding the energy. You will be open and able to see the bigger picture of your old ways and take responsibility for your part in things. You have experienced these old energies many times before, and this knowledge will help you to transcend your past so that the patterns stop repeating once and for all.

In the Records, you are using the energy of the spiral to unwind the feelings, beliefs, and patterns to heal. While you are unwinding, there's less resistance because the unwinding movement gains momentum which makes it easier to shift the energy.

Your intention is to unwind the spiral of feelings and cellular memory that is locked in your DNA. You may not know this, but your DNA holds onto the memory of any events that you are still emotional entangled with. Once you unwind anything you feel, you look at the Karma on the different levels (family, nation or race Karma) that you may be holding onto within this pattern and you unwind that as well. You also want to ask about the origin of the Karma and ask to unwind and release from the source.

Once you surrender into the process, it happens swiftly and quickly. The Akashic Records knows how to do the healing; you need to give it complete permission, both consciously and unconsciously.

If you feel like all of this is a lot, take a breath! Don't worry about the details; you need to let go and start exploring. You will build on this meditation in the next few chapters, and I will guide you step by step. This book is here to help you, and it will, so take a breath and let go.

Meditation: Step by Step

1. Intention

You always want to start with an overall intention before going into the Records. I have found when my clients use intentions in the Akashic Records they get the deepest healings and the best results. Making an intention is the easiest way to keep your focus and to get the best results for your life.

Your first intention should be simple. I suggest you start your first meditation with the intention to go into the Akashic Records in the Quantum Field and unwind an event from your childhood that still bugs you, but isn't a huge emotional event. Something small but impactful to you.

An example of this sort of event would be when the boy or girl you liked said something hurtful, or when you threw up in the elementary school classroom, or when a teacher called on you in class, and you froze up unable to answer. In other words, a memorable but minor event.

Select an event like this and set your intention to enter the Akashic Records in the Quantum Field and unwind it.

2. Relax your body

To relax your body, you are just going to close your eyes and take a few deep breaths.

3. Clear your thought forms and activate and align your chakras

In Chapter Four, you learned about thought forms and how they can get in the way if you are not careful. Having all your chakras aligned creates a coherence that allows your ego to take a back seat while you are in the Records. Before entering the Records, you will clear these thought forms out of the way and then activate and align your chakras, so you are ready to receive the deepest insight and healing.

In this step, you set the intention to do the meditation to clear your thought forms and activate and align your chakras which creates a coherence.

Once the thought forms clear and the chakras are activated and aligned, you should feel your heart expand and become the Toroidal Field around your body. That Torus is a moving vortex of energy, and when activated it opens up your consciousness and helps you connect to the Akashic Records.

4. Expand your heart into the Akashic Records

Your intention in this step is to expand beyond the Physical, Emotional and Mental planes into the Akashic Records on the Quantum Field. As you learned in Chapter Two, this creates a radical shift in what you can do in the Records.

Once you cohere in Step Three (above), you want to feel the heart center and allow it to expand out and become aware of your whole energy field as a Toroidal Field. Basically, you are expanding your consciousness. You want to expand your consciousness because your consciousness has unlimited energy and can easily become one with the Universe. Your consciousness has done this thousands of times. It has done it every time it has let go of your awareness of the physical body during sleep or in meditation.

Being cohered during this process from the previous step is essential since the ego mind will have less to say and your higher consciousness will follow the path it's used to and that it knows well.

You are expanding past your Physical bodies into the Universe, past the stars and planets into the Emotional Plane, into the Mental Plane, and then beyond these, into the Akashic Records on the Quantum Field.

You know you are there when you feel expanded, you don't see anything, and you feel calm. If you are questioning whether you are there or not, start all over again and cohere and expand. The ego is the only part of you that questions. Your soul or higher consciousness knows where it's going and what it's doing. So if you find yourself doubting, keep working on the foundational steps.

5. State your intention again

State your intention again from Step One (above) about what you want to do in the Records. As you do, the information available in the Records that serves your purpose will start to unfold around you. You will start to feel and sense the emotions and get the instant understanding of the bigger picture. It does not matter how the information comes through, just that you are open to receiving it. Now take your time and explore the Records that pertain to the event that you intend to clear.

6. Unwind the Emotions and Patterns

The greatest gift the Akashic Records can give to you is healing, and transcendence and the energy of the Toroidal spiral is how this healing happens. Once the feelings, Karmic patterns and mental images come up, *allow* them to unwind through the spiral energy (there is no need to force this unwinding). All the energy you give and receive comes through the Toroidal Field of the spiral around you. While allowing the old patterns to unwind, you will also want to recognize where you can take responsibility for the actions or feelings. You want to release things more deeply. Keep going over every aspect presented to you by the Records until you feel the emotions dissipate and you no longer feel the feelings previously attached to it.

7. Surrender

Now it is time to surrender the whole story, emotions, and past back into the Akashic Records, letting go is so important for your healing. It's not about giving up; it's about letting go. The energy of surrender will support the shift. In the energy of surrender, you are allowing the vibration of the Records to do its job of healing and recreating your past which helps to elevate the egos need to control the healing and helps you let go of any resistance that comes up, consciously or subconsciously.

8. Compassion

If you have any resistance to unwinding the energy or you still feel wronged or like you need to have the other person punished for what they did, then it is good to connect with compassion. Make the intention that you will see all sides of the event and connect to the feelings of compassion for you and anyone else affected by the experience. There is no reason why you should be impatient or hard on yourself as you process these deep things. Everyone was affected in some way, and everyone deserves compassion, even if their behavior was not ok.

9. Power of Joy

Now allow the power of joy to be present. Joy is the energy of gratitude and unconditional love, and when you are in the Akashic Records, the feelings of joy, gratitude, and love will wash all over you. Allow it to permeate into your cells and feel the Power of Joy through the vibration of gratitude and love. Become joy, gratitude, and love, and it will open you to the Divine within yourself.

10. Ask to be shown your Divine self

Are you ready to see your true potential beyond this limiting circumstance? Now that you have let it go and unwound the pattern begin to immerse yourself in your highest potential that is available to you now. Feel and be that energy without your thoughts getting in the way.

You can stay here as long as you want to absorb this way of being in your cells.

11. Become aware of the room you are in

Now come back to the here and now and open your eyes.

This entire process is much easier than it may seem. The best part about the Records is that once you start using the Akashic Records to receive healing, the steps of the meditation flow easier and faster.

Below is the full guided meditation. You may also go https://melissa-feick.com/rar-meditations/ and download the meditations.

GUIDED MEDITATION TO THE AKASHIC RECORDS

Your overall intention for this meditation is to go to the Akashic Records in the Quantum Field and unwind the past so you can master the Physical, Emotional and Mental planes.

Decide what Karmic pattern or blocks that you would like to unwind and make that your intention.

Close your eyes and get into a comfortable position.

Take three deep breaths. As you inhale, feel the breath move through your body, as you exhale release all tension and thoughts that may block your access to the Akashic Records.

Acknowledge your body and the energy in your cells.

Your next intention is to clear your thought forms and activate and align your chakras.

Bring your awareness to your heart chakra. Feel your breath as you breathe through the heart chakra area. Feel your heart expand with every intake of breath and a calm wash over you on the exhale.

Bring your awareness to the area around your shoulders and head. Notice all the chaos or chaotic thoughts, energy or feelings.

Your intention is to release all the thoughts that are stuck there. Become aware of any thoughts from yourself or ones you have picked up from others. See all of the thoughts lift off into the light. You are releasing their hold on you and releasing your attachment to them.

Once you sense the quietness, bring your awareness to the back of your head, where a girl would have a high ponytail or in the back of your third eye chakra. Notice the silence.

Bring your awareness to your heart and feel your heart expanding and opening.

Your intention is to align and activate your chakras.

Bring your awareness to your root chakra. Tell it to activate and feel your root chakra opening and activating.

Bring your awareness to your sacral chakra. Tell it to activate and feel your sacral chakra opening and activating.

Now your root chakra aligns with your sacral chakra.

Bring your awareness to your solar plexus chakra. Tell it to activate and feel your solar plexus chakra opening and activating.

Now your solar plexus aligns with your root and sacral chakras.

Bring your awareness to your heart chakra. Tell it to activate and feel your heart chakra opening and activating.

Now your heart chakra aligns with your root, sacral, and solar plexus chakras.

Bring your awareness to your throat chakra. Tell it to activate and feel your throat chakra opening and activating.

Now your throat chakra aligns with your root, sacral, solar plexus and heart chakras.

Bring your awareness to your third eye chakra. Tell it to activate and feel your third eye chakra opening and activating.

Now your third eye chakra aligns with your root, sacral, solar plexus, heart and throat chakras.

Bring your awareness to your crown chakra. Tell it to activate and feel your crown chakra opening and activating.

Now your crown chakra aligns with your root, sacral, solar plexus, heart, throat and third eye chakras.

Bring your awareness to your 8th chakra about a foot above your crown chakra. Tell it to activate and feel your 8th chakra opening and activating.

Now your 8th chakra aligns with your root, sacral, solar plexus, heart, throat, third eye and crown chakras.

Feel your energy activate, and your heart expands becoming the Toroidal Field around your body.

Your next intention is to expand your cohered consciousness through the levels of existence into the Quantum Field where the Akashic

Records reside. You will know you are in the Quantum Field when you are in the space of nothingness, and you feel love and connection.

There is nowhere to go. The Akashic Records are right here. All you need to do is surrender, feel your consciousness expanding and know that the intention is to connect to the Quantum Field in the Akashic Records.

Feel your consciousness expand. Feel the energy around your body.

Feel and become aware of the space around you.

Feel your consciousness expand and become one with the room you are in.

Feel and become aware of your consciousness expanding and become one with the Earth and feel the space around the Earth.

Feel your consciousness expand and become one with the Universe. Feel and become aware of the space around you.

Feel your consciousness expand and move past the Emotional and Mental planes into the Quantum Field of the Akashic Records.

Connect to your intention of what you chose to work on.

Connect with the event or past life and its connection to the pattern that you want to unwind.

Ask the living archives of the Akashic Records to assist and guide you.

You will get bits and chunks of information you will see, and it will be downloaded to you easily. You will be shown the players, patterns, and your part in the situations from a grander perspective. You may see past lives or important information which will help you transcend this issue.

Be open and surrender into the process.

Set the intention to unwind and heal the feelings of the event and all the cellular memory around it.

Allow the feelings, emotions, and any past trauma or anything you need to unwind in the Quantum Field. Once the energy clears, it rewrites the Akashic Records around that event. (Please don't try to control the rewriting. Allow the Records to do its job without you micromanaging it.)

While allowing the old patterns to unwind, you will also want to recognize where you can take responsibility for the actions or feelings. Keep going over every aspect until you feel it's resolved and you no longer feel the feelings attached to it.

If new feelings or visions come up, be present with them and allow them to unwind.

Now surrender the story, patterns, and feelings into the Quantum Field. Allow the Quantum Field to take care of anything else around this situation.

So you are surrendering the past into the Quantum Field.

Stay expanded and connected to the Akashic Records and the Quantum Field.

Your intention is to feel gratitude for the possibilities that will become present now that the past has transcended. Doing this keeps your heart open and allows healing to happen organically.

Now you may choose to feel compassion for everyone involved, including yourself.

Feel the gratitude and allow the gratitude to fill your energy.

Stay in the Quantum Field while being in the energy of gratitude.

This will create new possibilities for you.

If you see anything or start thinking, surrender the thought and be in the gratitude again.

Allow the energy of gratitude to permeate your energy, the energy of the Akashic Records, the energy of the Quantum Field, and all the cells in your body.

Allow the gratitude to vibrate in your cells and become one with you.

Your next intention is that everything you have done in this meditation has already healed, been recreated, and is part of your life now.

This new energy of who you are is already available to you. You may open your living a new story, and you will be a person who is open and willing to experience a new future.

When you are ready, open your eyes.

CHAPTER 10

SOUL PATH

For centuries mystics, philosophers and spiritual leaders have tried to describe the soul and the soul's voice. Only you will know what *your* soul or higher consciousness sounds like, but be assured that it *is* there, guiding you. Everyone's soul voice is guiding them. The voice of the soul or higher consciousness speaks to you in a whisper. You do not have to listen. Every conscious being has free will to listen or not. It may not be something you are consciously aware of all of the time, but you've probably had moments when you felt the connection with your soul.

Your soul is always communicating with you and giving you signs. When you connect to your soul, you feel surer of your path, and you are in the flow of life. If you take a moment and reflect on the times when your life moved like a beautiful dance and everything fell into perfect order, you will discover how your soul spoke to you.

You are on a journey, and there is no wrong or right way to go about your journey. Everyone else is on a journey, too, but it will never look the same as yours. This path, the one that you are on now, is always up to you, and you get to choose each step that you take. That is your free will. One way to look at the path or journey you are on in this lifetime is to see it as the soul path, or part of the journey of your soul. You can think of this journey or soul path as the reason you are here, living a life on Earth, fulfilling your higher purpose, but no matter what you call it, the most important thing is that it's *your* journey.

SOUL PATH AND REINCARNATION

Right now you are in a physical body, and at one point the physical body will no longer function. Like all physical things, it doesn't last forever. Eventually, the body can no longer house the soul, and the soul leaves the body.

People are a lot like hermit crabs. When a hermit crab outgrows its shell, it then ventures out of the old shell and finds a new one. When you pass on to the other side, you are more conscious and, luckily, you have assistance in finding your new body or shell. When your spirit is transitioning, you are also very discerning when it comes to finding a new home to house your soul. The body must meet some important criteria.

You are here to master the mental, emotional and physical body which is attached to the dense Earthly world and the illusion connected to it. The experiences you have in a human body are different from those experiences you would have as a consciousness with a purely vibrational energy body. Once you start incarnating on Earth, you will probably keep coming back to new bodies until you have mastered this energy system on the Physical Plane. Since you, like many others, are coming back lifetime after lifetime, you choose different bodies with the help of your Spiritual Council.

YOUR SPIRITUAL COUNCIL

You are not alone in your existence, no one is. Luckily everyone has helpers on the other side. These beings guide and direct us when we choose to incarnate (like when you chose to come into this life) and after we leave an incarnation. They are around you, but they usually aren't interfering in your life.

The Akashic Records can help connect you with many different kinds of Guides. Some of these wise beings guide you from what is called your Spiritual Council. You have a Spiritual Council that is made up of advanced souls. They have to be more advanced than you are to be able to guide you. Your council can have between three to twelve beings on it. Every human has a Council, and you meet with them when you pass over to the other side, and they always assist you in your life review. They have been called many names, but most call them the Council of Elders or the Wise Council.

Your Council has been guiding you for many lifetimes. Sometimes they will ask other guides to intervene in your life and help you by sending you messages through people, guides or synchronicities. Most humans are unaware of how to fully utilize their Council throughout their life, and so they are at a disadvantage, navigating life through trial and error.

Your Council is there to guide you while you are in the Akashic Records to help you navigate, heal and transcend your negative patterns or issues. They are there to assist you in taking responsibility and healing your Karmic patterns, as detailed in Chapters Seven and Eight.

The council guides you, but you also play a role. For example, when you are in the Records, your Spiritual Council will steer you toward the awareness of how the pattern of abandonment has kept you safe and how you've abandoned others, so they don't get too close to you. Their job is to bring the information to your awareness, but it's up to you to come up with the answers and take responsibility to heal it. You would never be able to transcend the Karmic pattern if your Council did all the work for you!

Since the Records are a living energy connected with the Divine, anyone can access them and utilize them. Your Spiritual Council are wise, and they have access to all of your Akashic Records, past, present and future, but they are not in charge of the Records. They know your past Karma, relationships and all information about your lifetimes. This Council knows why you came to Earth and why you have certain interactions or connections with specific people.

Your Council is there to assist you in your big life decisions, but there are certain decisions or choices you're supposed to make on your own. It's best not to give your power away to the Records or your Council by asking for guidance about mundane situations. The Records are for healing, which you can use anytime, but asking your Council for guidance is helpful when you use the information for transcendence and healing. The Records can create major life changes, so asking about things that don't matter on the soul level, like if the boy next door is in love with you, is like using a sports car as a flower pot. You'd be using your resources in a limited way, and you'd be missing out on the best part!

When you work with your Spiritual Council in the Akashic Records and start to heal yourself, you can accelerate your spiritual progress on your soul's mission. While in the Records you won't see your Council and they usually don't interact with you, but they will lovingly guide the process within the Records.

The key to working in the Akashic Records is to be super inquisitive about yourself, your issues and your healing. Your Council isn't interested in making the process within the Records about them. They can guide and assist you without needing to be seen or heard.

Most people you know will only connect to this Wise Council after death, but you can utilize them now, in the Akashic Records. When you are in the Records, you can ask your Council for guidance. Ask to allow the wisdom of your Council to guide you and assist you in working with the Records themselves. They want you to evolve, and they know you as a soul very, very well. They only have the best intentions for you. How wonderful would it be to work through all the negative Karma now and not have to regret wasting a lifetime being stuck in the same unhappy patterns, over and over again!

MY SPIRITUAL COUNCIL

Not long ago, I had to make a major decision about my life. I have been blessed to be married to an amazing man for about 24 years, and we have two beautiful children together. Although my husband is a wonderful person, I started to recognize as time went on, that some things were no longer working in our relationship. It was a pattern that didn't feel right.

I have always believed that there are times when relationships fall away, and this seemed to be one of those times. Even though I'd been with the same person for over 20 years, something changed, and it didn't seem right anymore. There is much more to this story, but I had to decide between staying in my marriage and giving it my all or choosing to leave.

As I was intensely asking this question in my life, I used the Records to help me decide. Over the course of a few months, I went to my Spiritual Council in the Akashic Records and asked different questions about my relationship, my children, and my family. Believe it or not, *I never asked, "Should I leave my husband?"* I asked things like, "What will I learn if I stay?" "Will I grow if I stay?" "What will be better for my husband?" "How will my teenage daughter and college-age son's life trajectory change?" Notice how *none* of these questions are asking if I should or should not split from my husband. That kind of question would be giving my power away. It was my decision. All of these questions are about what may happen depending on what choices I make. I have free will, and my choices are mine.

My family members also have their own free will. Even if the Records showed me a few possibilities of how these choices will affect my family, they still have a choice in how they react to the situation and what they do with their life. For me, working with the Records and asking these questions helped to understand my options on a deeper level, like how it will affect the people in my life.

I would never give my power away to my Spiritual Council and do what I *think* they are telling me to do. What I do in my life is always my choice. I have every right to take into account what I'm shown or told and make my decision from that place. For something this big, there are a lot of things to consider, so as I worked with the Council and Records, I was not blindly following orders. Instead, I thoughtfully considered all the information as I asked questions about all areas of the decision. I was also looking for areas that I might need to heal and Karma I needed to transcend. I was open to seeing where I needed to take responsibility for patterns. I knew that if there were Karma that I needed to transform, and I left him without unwinding my Karma, then I would end up recreating that pattern in another relationship. It could be any relationship: business partner, friend, or client. If I didn't heal that Karma, then it would just come back so no matter what I decided, I was committed to working on whatever Karma was involved in the situation.

Here is one example of how my personal Council has helped me with my life, and I believe that my life is more peaceful and flows easier because of working with them and the Akashic Records on the Quantum Field.

REINCARNATION

Reincarnation is a cycle of birth and death. It's also called the Wheel of Life, which is appropriate when you think about the ups and downs associated with life. As you start to go to the Records, you will have a deeper understanding of reincarnation and especially your soul path in this lifetime. You will discover so much about your ego creation and how the soul is trying to lead you past your ego and into the Oneness of your fullest potential.

Each time someone reincarnates, their Spiritual Council assists them in choosing the family that best matches the Karmic patterns they are working through. This way when you reincarnate, the family experiences and opportunities presented to you will bring the best options to transcend the illusion. The Akashic Records hold all the information from each incarnation and the experiences you've had as a soul. Like all of us, you are here to master the Physical, Emotional and Mental planes and bodies, so one of the reasons we incarnate is to discover the depth of information available on Earth and how the ego navigates the Physical Plane. If you would like more information about reincarnation, I have included two books from MD's who studied reincarnation. [5] [6]

REINCARNATION AND RELATIONSHIPS

You have relationships for a reason, to assist you in your growth. You have the opportunity to grow from every person that comes into your life. You agreed to connect with certain people in your life so you may transcend and evolve. Every relationship you have can keep you stuck

---

[5] Book: Children Who Remember Previous Lives: A Question of Reincarnation by Ian Stevenson, MD

[6] Book: Life Before Life: A Scientific Investigation of Children's Memories of Previous Lives by Jim Tucker, MD

in Karma or help you transcend. It's up to you, not the other person, to transcend your Karma.

If you are here to learn about your Karma and soul growth, working on your relationships is the best way to do that. You can learn so much about yourself through your interactions with others. Even if you start connecting with different people, you will repeat the negative patterns of your relationships with others until you have healed yourself.

The real truth is that you are not here to learn negative lessons. You are here to evolve and transcend. The easiest and fastest way to do this is to become fully aware of your patterns in your life and your relationships and work on them in the Akashic Records.

SOUL EVOLUTION

Every soul is on a mission to expand and evolve. The soul has free will on how it will develop and grow. You can only grow if you become more and more self-aware. You can do this through your work in the Records, if you are open to it, and take personal responsibility. You will become more aware of your part in your relationships, more aware of your dramas and less attached to all of it. The real growth happens in the healing process as you become less attached to that old cycle.

Your growth creates many ripple effects. As you transcend and evolve, you raise your consciousness and your vibration, which then opens you up to see past the illusion and into the Oneness.

Soul evolution is not about fixing the soul or for it to evolve as the frog evolves from a tadpole. Because you are familiar with these models on the Physical Plane, you might think spiritual growth works the same way. Soul evolution is a different kind of transcendence that gets richer and deeper every time you grow. The soul is witnessing the experience of your human decisions and is a part of the experience at the same time. Your job here is to evolve and transcend. A quick, easy way to advance your soul evolution is to work with the Records. Perhaps this is more than you ever thought possible!

CHAPTER 11

REALITY, EGO, AND THE BRAIN

What is Reality? Working with the Akashic Records will give you new ways of looking at the world around you. Information from science and spirituality can help you to watch out for illusions created by the ego so that you can see more of what is really around you. As you advance your consciousness, you will perceive everything in entirely new ways: ways that are all true! Keep reading to understand Reality, Ego, and the Brain more in-depth.

Coming to understand reality has been part of a long personal journey of mine. I remember how in the mid-1990's my first spiritual teachers started talking about reality and how everything is a reflection of our beliefs. It was a new theory for me and others in our class. They spoke about illusion, what they called the 'matrix of creation' and how the matrix creates everything. They told me that the matrix is a geometric shape and these geometric shapes make up all of creation. It was so fascinating, and this concept blew my mind, but I don't think I understood it at that time.

I started to study The Course in Miracles in the early 2000's with a different teacher, and the notion of reality started to sink in.

But to be perfectly honest, it wasn't until I started experiencing and meditating in the Quantum Field that I could understand reality. The information in this chapter was born from all of that work.

EGO

In understanding reality, you first need to understand the ego. We understand the world through our ego and our brain. You've read about illusion in Chapter Seven. The ego creates and connects to the illusion.

The ego cannot see reality for what it truly is because it believes in the physical world and physical senses. It believes that what the eyes see is real and that you should be fearful of anything you can't understand. Studies show that what our eyes perceive can be deceiving.[7]

Lifetime after lifetime you're recalibrating your experiences and either perpetuating old emotional and mental habits or overcoming them. The more you transcend the old self or ego self, the more of your higher consciousness *becomes* you in the physical body. The goal of reincarnation is to shed the ego identity and become the ascended master. To understand your soul's path, you will need to look at the ego's path.

THE EGO'S PATH

The Native Americans and other indigenous cultures will insist that you are connected and one with everything around you. They will say that what you do will have an impact on what happens to the world around you. So this creates big questions to ask about the connection

---

[7] http://www.sciencealert.com/how-your-eyes-deceive-you

between yourself and the world. Are we one or are we separate beings? Which one is it? Are we in a physical reality here or are we spiritual energy that expands beyond all that we can see on Earth?

Your ego feels separate and your soul and your spirit experience One-ness. The soul and spirit are your truest nature. Think of the ego as a person trying to control you and the environment around you. The ego does not have a sense of control as you connect to your truth, which is Oneness, and thus your true self. Your ego prefers for you to be separate, for, in the separation, the ego is in complete control and keeps you entangled in the illusion of this world. The illusion feels dense, while Oneness feels light.

For you to transcend the lower planes and transcend the illusion, you will need to see through the ego's identity, and it's attachment to the illusion. It is the attachment that creates suffering. As you work in the Records, you want to keep asking to transcend the illusion and the Karma which cause suffering.

While you are healing in the Records, your ultimate goal is to release the lower energies and Karma so you can become more connected to the Oneness. Being in the Oneness will help you to see the truth of your reality and just how powerful you are. It's the ego that holds us back from reaching those higher states of consciousness.

REALITY

Reality is all about the perception you place on your experiences and your outer world. You are constantly projecting your thoughts, feelings, and ideas into the space around you. As you project the thoughts, feelings, and ideas, those energies connect to the Quantum Field, and the Field arranges for the energetic match to show up in your life. Through this projection of your thoughts and feelings, you create your reality.

The Law of Magnetism states that we are creating our reality through what we put out there because we attract more of the same to us.

Since the Akashic Records contain a recording of all you have experienced from across all time and space, past, present and future, you can create improvements in your experience of reality from working in the Records. You are not destined to live in the past. The Records can help you to expand your awareness past the limited ego self and allow you to become your fullest potential.

When you access the Akashic Records on the Quantum Field, you heal past wounds through transcending old patterns, and you start to create a new reality for yourself! The new reality is one of the greatest gifts of the Records, for you to recognize your ability to consciously create the life you desire!

PAST LIVES

Going into past lives can help you heal very quickly. When you address any part of your past, it will help you to unwind Karma, and imagine how powerful a shift would be if you've carried a pattern through multiple lifetimes. That is a lot of years living and interacting with reality in the same stuck way. But it doesn't have to stay stuck—that's where the Records come in.

When you are accessing your Akashic Records or reading another's Records, you may see one or more past lives. Most times, the information about the past life will come to you in an instant, and you will understand how it relates to your question or pattern. This lifetime or lifetimes are coming up for a reason, so you may notice the patterns, feelings, and situations, and recognize how it relates to you now.

You will only see the past lives in which you need to understand the feelings, thoughts or behaviors which relate to the pattern you've been trying to shed. Before you came into being, you chose the life you are living now to transcend these old patterns. You are not working in the Records to reinforce your lower emotional patterns. Instead, you may heal and transcend them, see the illusion and create the life you desire.

If you are talking about a past life like a juicy story of betrayal and intrigue to explain drama going on, i.e., that is why your ex is such an asshole, then you are missing out on the healing aspect of the Akashic Records. You're not stuck with the way past lives have set things up for you. You are not a victim to your past lives. You get to do something new. You are not here to recreate the past; you already lived that life. You are experiencing the past life in the Records, so you can unwind the past *pattern* and become the more Divine aspect of yourself. When you unwind the past pattern, you start to live in the now, the reality, which creates a more loving, abundant future!

My Client, Joseph, had an issue with feeling stuck in life. As we worked together, I saw a pattern of feeling trapped and, together, we decided to look into it. This pattern was not only in his life but it was also a pattern from his family. He realized that in his family everyone had to live up to certain expectations. Many members of his family felt stuck, feeling like they had to be a certain way. Even their aspirations of what or who they had to be felt very limited and fixed within his family. There was also resistance to this pattern, of not wanting to accept the boxes placed on each of them. Joe felt the resistance to having to work hard to prove his worth. That resistance hurt his career, but he still felt the pressure of feeling trapped by it, so it was a no-win situation.

While I was in the Records, I found this pattern, and we began unwinding and healing Joseph's past, together. During the reading, while gathering all the information about this pattern, I also saw a few lifetimes that had a direct Karmic relation to this feeling of being stuck.

One of them was where his body was stuck in a crevice in a cave, and he was trapped there.

When I see something relating to a past life, a family pattern, and a client's pattern, all at once the Akashic Records will automatically start to unwind and heal the whole Karmic pattern. The pattern is part of a matrix of energy that begins to shift as Joseph sees the pain and issues this has caused in his life. It comes from his awareness that something beyond his surroundings and the illusion he sees through, his ego, is at work here. When he can see how it plays out in a wider spiritual pattern, it's easier for him to let go of the Karma keeping everything in place.

This reading was a major shift in Joseph's life. Afterward, he no longer felt trapped and started to feel more empowered. He could live another way. In fact, his understanding of the world around him changed because he was viewing the world from a higher consciousness. He knew he has the opportunity to live another way and break the pattern. He is free, and this is why the Akashic Records are so powerful!

You create your reality, and sometimes people have created realities that do not serve them. You don't have to do that anymore, but first, you have to be aware that you are creating this. Just because you may have had sad or painful things happen on the level of your family or in a past life, does not mean that you are destined to recreate that forever. You are stuck in the reality that you are still suffering the pain and sorrow of your past. If that is how you choose to see reality, you can keep living that way, or you can decide to do something new. If you are interested in transformation, then your intention in the Records should be to transcend the reality of suffering. You are letting go of the emotional ties, the Karmic entanglement, and the trauma so you can create differently.

How You Create Your Reality

I have heard thousands of stories from clients and the common thread from all these stories is that these people are living in the past. Research about the brain can give you insight into why this is so common. Every day you have 50,000 to 70,000 thoughts running around in your head. No wonder you are exhausted! Researchers say that this number is a conservative estimate. But if that surprises you, then it may blow your mind to know what the fascinating part about all of these thoughts truly is: 90-98% of what runs through your mind on a daily basis are the same thoughts that you thought yesterday! When I heard this, I said, "What??!!?". The ego wants you to buy into the fact that you are extremely intelligent and that your thoughts are very important. You are a thinking person, "I think. Therefore I am," but in reality, the thoughts you are thinking are most likely working against you. The highest percentage of the time, almost all the time, your thoughts are looping through your subconscious thought patterns.

Buddhists have an ancient teaching called 'habitual tendencies' which can include habitual thoughts. They believe that the thoughts you think on a regular basis are habitual and are usually negative. The Buddhists also believed that if you keep thinking the same habitual thoughts, then you will bring them back lifetime after lifetime. They understood that if you don't transcend them, they won't leave you. Think about it; if this is true, you may have thought the same thoughts for *thousands* of years.

The truth is that your thoughts matter. They don't just serve to make you miserable; they shape your life. Since thoughts and feelings create your reality, every thought you have creates some part of the reality you experience in your daily life. You can see this happen for other people as well. When I was a teenager, my friend's sister, who was in her 20's, would sometimes hang out with us. I started to notice her habit of saying over and over, "there's something wrong in my female area." She went to many doctors who told her nothing was wrong. Around that time, I told my friend, "Your sister is going to have issues in that area because that's all she talks about." Back then I hadn't even studied anything about reality and creation, but I did know, on some level, that she would create what she wanted. Because she kept talking about it, I knew that she wanted to have a problem in her 'female area,' and within two years she did.

You are consistently creating your experience and your life. That is the nature of reality. Your thoughts have an enormous impact on your life because they are reflected in your experience very quickly. I have told my clients for years that this moment is creating your next moment, so what are you thinking and where is your focus right now?

To become aware of your thoughts is a powerful practice, but it is one that takes time to build, and it never stops. To be mindful will become a discipline that you will have to revisit over again and the Akashic Records will help to draw your awareness to places you have been ignoring. Remember you always have the power to change, but this awareness and mindfulness must happen first. The Buddhist philosophy around what they call Mindfulness is that it is a way of life to be mindful of every aspect of your existence, from what you eat, to how you treat others, what you think about, and how you feel.

Many people do not do this work. Most people go through life unconsciously. Studies by cognitive neuroscientists have shown that 80-95% of your waking life you are living from the unconscious or subconscious mind. You are just reacting to the world around you from the instinctual or habitual parts of your brain. These subconscious reactions include your thoughts, but also your feelings and behavior patterns, like why you buy certain things. You're not thinking about any of the choices you are making because you are going on autopilot, exactly like you have in the past. No wonder many people find themselves re-living the same sort of life every day.

If you want your life to change, then the information in this chapter may be a big wake up call for you. You might want your life to change, but if you are not present with your thoughts and feelings, then you are just recreating the same experience you had yesterday, including the same thoughts you had yesterday and the same feelings you had yesterday. Yesterday you had the same thoughts and feelings you had the day before that. Most likely you are experiencing the same thoughts and feelings you've had since you were a young child and possibly ones that you had lifetimes ago. Sometimes I have a small desire to give people a little shake, like "Wake up! There is more to life!"

Aren't you ready for a nice change? Isn't it time to take back your power and start to create the life you want? Please say yes! I know what it's like to have an amazing life and I would love for you to join me there with the others who have done this work. It's a ton more fun on this side, I promise you, and it's worth becoming aware of your habitual patterns.

The Akashic Records will help you recognize the habitual thought and feeling patterns and help you to transcend them. A side effect of working in the Records is that they will give you more clarity on things you couldn't even see before, including patterns you've experienced for a long time. You'll see them in a new way, and be able to release them. Once they are released, you can get past your blocks to feel the possibilities of the life you desire and become more aware of your highest potential! It's an exciting opportunity to make radical changes very easily and very quickly.

Change your thoughts, and you will change your reality. Reality is made up of energy waves. Your thoughts and feelings are vibrations. Those vibrations are sent out into the Quantum Field. The Quantum Field is the energy of all possibilities, and I mean ALL! Once those vibrations are sent out to the Quantum Field, it reacts immediately, almost as if it says, "Oh, that's what he wants," and sends something to match the vibration back to you. The Quantum Field doesn't judge what you put out. It doesn't see anything like a good or bad energy or feeling; it's just a vibrational frequency to the Field. You pick that vibration, and then you receive its match. If you aren't consciously choosing because you are running your patterns, you still receive something back from the Quantum Field, but it probably is more of the same thing you've always received.

My understanding of reality has evolved. For many years I have been meditating and connecting to the Quantum Field, but I didn't have a name for what that was. At first, I called it 'the Oneness,' or 'the Expansiveness of Pure Unconditional Love.' I now realize that what I have been connecting to all along is the Quantum Field. The Quantum Field is made up of unconditional love and pure potential. Responding to the vibrations that you send out is incredibly loving, even if you feel like you don't like your life the way it is. The Field loves you enough to send you what you desire every time, which means that the Quantum Field is responding to the unconscious thoughts and feelings that you send to the Quantum Field about what you desire.

You have to do more than recite verbal affirmations to tell the Quantum Field what you desire. You need to connect to the feelings and thoughts that match your desires. Then you'll get receive what you want. For example, if you are saying the words, "I want a soul mate who loves me," but, in contrast, you are also feeling anger and resentment toward your ex, then the Quantum Field of Pure Love responds more to the feelings of anger and resentment. The Field speaks thoughts and feelings and doesn't understand verbal words.

Take another example. I had a client that had recently left her husband and was looking for love everywhere. She would obsessively think and talk about one guy after another, but each relationship, no matter how long or short it was, would end the same way: failure. Then she would become depressed and start all over again with someone new. What I tried to explain to her is that she was living her old story of victimization and her need for love. She was interacting with different people, but her habitual thoughts and feelings were creating similar situations over and over again. She could become aware of those patterns and transform them, and she'd probably create a different result of feeling loved in her life, whether she ended up with the perfect guy or not.

If you're feeling stuck, there are things you can do to help yourself get out of the past and your old story. When you are in the Akashic Records, ask to see the pattern involved with the situation and ask how to heal it. Ask to see the situation and story differently and unwind all old trauma patterns. When you do this healing in the Akashic Records, it will release old wounds in the cellular memory and rewire the *neural pathways* in the brain. That means that you will be changing your thoughts and feelings about it. You will be able to do something new, and think or feel in new ways—not just your old patterns.

The old hurt feelings of the past and the old ways of thinking are just a story. Once you start experiencing different lifetimes in the Records, you will notice that all these lifetime stories are the same basic story. You do not have to keep living the same experience over and over again, lifetime after lifetime. Take back your life and your power back and choose to experience your life differently! Start small and work your way up to big changes, even a little shift can have huge ripple effects.

THE EGO AND YOUR TRUE PURPOSE

In Chapter One you learned that everyone's Soul Purpose is to transcend the illusion and the ego's delusion so that you can better express love, and become the energy of equanimity. You are here on this Earth to know and understand the ego and the ego's voice. You are here to experience. Each experience you have can draw you into the ego and separation, or it can expand your awareness and higher consciousness. You get to choose! That's the exciting thing. You always have choices even if you don't like your choices. Working with the Records can help you to make choices that expand your awareness and allow you to let go of things that are holding you back.

Your potential to reach higher vibrations is always available to you, but while you connect to the feelings and thoughts your ego produces, you know only separation, suffering, and drama. The ego's desire to hold onto fear and trauma is what keeps you from recognizing your true identity. The ego truly believes that *it is the only identity*. The truth is that the *you* of your ego, separate from everything and everyone else, doesn't exist. Your truth is to connect to all that is, in the Quantum Field, a state of pure love and Oneness. The ego loves scandalous pain and suffering so that it may hold on to the illusions that are present on the Earth plane. The ego doesn't want you to let go, even if it means you have to hold onto the pain of the past and keep reliving the same cycles over and over again. Your real identity is more than that; it's happier and less sad. The Records can help you loosen the tie to the ego so you can feel better in your own skin every day and experience less drama.

The ego's existence depends upon both your conscious thoughts and your unconscious thoughts. It drives the desire to be special and important. As humans, we see ourselves as separate and believe that we are superior beings in this world. All of us are part of the same energy, and we connect to everything through the Quantum Field. We are all equal. This space of equanimity is peaceful and safe because you are always loved no matter what or who you are. It feels better, even if it scares your ego to release the feeling of being separate and special. Everybody is special and not unique at the same time.

The ego loves opposites and extremes because it believes in the duality of the Physical Plane. The ego will either tell you that you are wonderful, or it will put you down. It keeps you stuck in the illusion and perception that *everything around you is more important than connecting to your true identity on the inside.* In other words, the ego is looking outward, into the world, to feel love and connection from somewhere else, outside of the Divine. The Records will help you to see your true power and potential and helps you to connect with higher states of consciousness like Oneness, connection, inner peace and Divine love. While the ego will guide you to continue to chase things in the future, the Quantum Field will help you to connect to the positive feelings you desire right now at this very moment. You don't have to wait.

The ego is the part of you that loves to look at and reflect on your image, like looking through a mirror or thinking about what other people see in you. The ego is a self-conscious understanding of your knowledge of yourself as an individual. It sees itself through its surroundings or the things outside itself. It is a part of your identity on Earth, but the ego persona isn't who you truly are. Once you start to transcend your Karma, your ego tends to be less prevalent in your life.

You can't fault the ego; its main concern is the preservation of the self and its control over its environment. The ego is trying to keep you safe, and it is just doing its job. The ego is part of the animal brain of reaction and self-preservation. That part of your brain is responsible for the fight, flight, freeze and hide response. This response keeps you in a place of unconscious reaction. You cannot use your higher thinking when you are in this reactionary mode. The ego uses the fear of the animal brain and illusion to project fear into your environment. That fear can show up as a phobia or fear of the unknown. Many people also experience it as anxiety.

Perhaps the ego used to be more useful in the past, but it is probably not serving you now. The problem is that the ego is continuing to work the same way it used to before. The ego has an obsession with the story. It will exaggerate and add to a story about situations going on so that it feels safe and *feels connected to the story*. The story makes a kind of sense that allows the ego to feel in control and understand the world, even if the story is harmful like, "It's all my fault," or "I don't have any control." Its desire to connect with people is powerful and may even make the story sound more appealing to people close by to preserve relationships with them. For instance, it may feel safer for the ego to play the victim in a story so that other people will provide love. The story becomes connected to the way the ego understands its value and receives love and attention. It feels safer in the story.

Think about a time when people were sharing these ego stories with others close by, in your experience. Have you ever noticed that when one person's ego is speaking to another, they keep trying to one-up each other's story? They want to show that their story was more difficult or painful than the other person's story. The ego needs to control and manipulate because that makes the ego feel like it's safe in the world. That's why the ego doesn't like for someone else to get more attention and will assert its story to feel superior.

The ego is attached to the human body and the senses of the human body, so you have to work on every level to address it. You can only overcome the ego when you have worked through the physical, emotional and mental issues that keep you feeling separate and alone. Your ego comes back with 'you' lifetime after lifetime until you have mastered this on the Physical, Emotional and Mental planes and bodies, just like the habitual thoughts mentioned before. Overcoming the ego on all of these levels is easy to do while in the Akashic Records on the level of the Quantum Field because it is a very high vibration.

Once you have mastered the lower energies, you no longer need the ego or the ego's identity. You will never feel separate since you see beyond the illusion of separation and live consistently in the Oneness.

As you do this work, be sure to feel into what is the right pace for you. Sometimes if you try to overthrow all of these ego patterns in one fell swoop, you will have a lot of resistance or backlash. I tell people not to try to kill off the ego because I have seen many people on their spiritual path try to kill off the ego and their ego resists. Those sorts of people usually have the biggest egos, as well, and they love to tell you how they don't have an ego. Watch any traps the ego sets like that. You'll probably have to acknowledge your limitations as a human being like the rest of us and keep doing the work!

Your best bet is to spend lots of time in the Akashic Records healing and transcending your lower self so you can become connected to your higher consciousness. Once you are living consistently in the Oneness, you will need less and less connection with the ego self. You'll provide your own sense of safety, and won't need those ego traps to survive.

How the Brain is Wired

I have a fascination with the brain and psychology. In college, I took a class on neuropsychology, and that was my first introduction to the 'neural pathways' in the brain. Imagine a brain lighting up with different electrical impulses. Each impulse sends information or triggers thoughts, feelings or movement in the body. The neural pathways are like crevices or ditches in the brain. These electrical or hormonal signals follow along the ditches like a highway to send a signal from the brain to the body, telling it what to do.

Over time, these *neural pathways* get deeper and deeper the more times the same kind of signals fire. The signals follow the path of least resistance. Remember those habitual thoughts people tend to think unconsciously? Those habitual thoughts follow ingrained neural pathways. The habitual thoughts are why it is hard for people to change a behavior, thought or feeling. The ditch (neural pathway) for that pattern becomes deeper with time, and the flow of the signal tends to fall more and more into the same pathway.

Think of the flow of your thoughts and feelings moving down neural pathways as like a stream of water created from melting snow coming down a mountain. Every spring thaw, the stream comes down and creates a pathway to the bottom of the snowy mountain. Each time the snow melts, the stream takes the same route down the mountain because previous thaws have formed a crevice there. It becomes the easiest route, getting deeper and smoother each time, which makes it even easier for the water to flow there. The brain is the same; it takes the pathway of least resistance. As your thoughts and feelings start to become a habit, it's like that stream becomes stronger, creating a deeper river bed bit by bit. Your thoughts will naturally start to channel along the neural pathways created by past thoughts, feelings, and neural signals.

You have patterns of thinking that create the same situations over and over again. You create the same reality with different players. The people, situations, and experiences may be a little different, but you are experiencing the same relationships with them. Note how heavy that feels. It doesn't have to be that way. Through the Akashic Records, you can let go of your past and do something new. You can change your thoughts and feelings to create a different future. You'll create a new future more easily because you are no longer living the same patterns and working those neural pathways as you did in the past. You'll transcend them.

They have discovered that the brain has neuroplasticity which means the brain and the ditches (neural pathways) are malleable and can change or heal. Since the brain is malleable through the neuroplasticity, the brain is not hard-wired to your past. It can be rewired and recreated. That's good news!

To start making a change, you begin with awareness. You have to recognize your unhealthy patterns to change them, and the fastest way to do that is through the Akashic Records. In the Akashic Records you can view the whole picture and unwind or release all the old feelings, beliefs, and stories all at once! Other healing modalities only work on one of these levels, but in the Records on the level of the Quantum Field, the intention is to release *all* of it.

Becoming aware of your unhealthy patterns in the Records will be the first step to clearing them. Following the instructions from Chapter Nine, you'll be able to unwind and heal the Karma involved in those situations. Then each time you release the old patterns, emotions, beliefs, and stories driving the unhappiness in your life, you'll be more connected to your higher consciousness. From this place, you can transform your life. You will recognize the old self no longer serves you because you shifted the old neural pathways into new neural pathways.

Changing your neural pathways because of the work in the Akashic Records on the Quantum Field returns you to your *natural* state. Your natural state of consciousness as a human being is actually to be in the Higher States of Awareness like Unconditional Love, Compassion, Joy, Oneness, Inner Peace, etc. When you are resisting these higher states of consciousness, it's because you want to live in the past. You may say you want to change, but you have to take the time to go to the Records and commit to changing.

Enjoy the radical new ways to change your way of thinking and get out of a rut, literally, as you change the structure of your brain to match the life you want to be living. You don't need to live unconsciously anymore. You have access to the Akashic Records. From here, there are only endless possibilities. Freedom to think and feel the way you want to will lead to manifesting and creating whatever it is you want in life.

CHAPTER 12

READING THE
AKASHIC RECORDS FOR OTHERS

Not only can you transform your own life with everything you've learned so far about the Akashic Records, but with a few additional skills, you can also help others. Since the Akashic Records holds all information for everyone in our Universe, it is easy to help others by reading their Akashic Records for them. Reading for others allows you to share valuable information, as well as helps other people to connect to beneficial energy held in the Records to assist in their transformation. As you read for them, you may find yourself guided to help them by connecting with their Spiritual Council (mentioned in Chapter Ten).

Through the chapter, I will also share things I've learned from my professional experience. I've provided readings and healings for thousands of people throughout my many years of practice. I hope this information helps you to be of service to others and to share your light in the easiest way possible. Connecting to the Records will help you to change the world, one transformation at a time. Working with others will also deepen the transformations you experience in your life, as well.

Getting Permission to Access the Records for Others

Reading for others is different than reading for yourself because it involves another person's freedom and choice. When you read for yourself, you choose to access your Records, and you choose how deep you will go. Before you read for another person, even if they are present with you, you must honor that the other person is the one who decides if you can read for them. These are their Records, not yours.

Note: Before you do any readings for another person there is built-in ethical energy in the Akashic Records, and you may only do readings for someone who permits you. You may not read the records to manipulate or control anyone. Readings are for the evolution of the soul you are helping. Assuming you have permission, this chapter will teach you how to give Akashic Records readings for other people.

As you start to read the Records for others, you may receive information about your client's relationships or the client may ask a question about other people in his or her life. For example, you might get some information about a client's relationship with his wife, or the client may ask you something about her, and this can get tricky. The other person is not there to give permission, so you can't go into the wife's Records directly. In this case, there is still a way that you can provide some clarity to your client without actually going into the Records and reading for someone without their permission. What you can do is go into your client's Akashic Records and see what will happen in their relationship or see information that can answer their question about the relationship. The relationship has its own Record. Because in a way you are reading the relationship Records, this is different than going into a random person's Records and asking about them. The same thing goes for your relationships. Should you choose to ask the Records for guidance about your relationships, make sure, your intention is to read information about the relationship, not the other person if they have not permitted you to read for them. Although, you will receive all the information you need by reading your Records or your clients' Records and relationship Records.

Once again, in learning how to give readings for others, you must obtain verbal permission first. You cannot connect to anyone's Records unless you have that verbal permission to do so. As with all rules, there are always exceptions.

The notable exception to this rule is if you feel called to do a reading for your young child, or if you want to do a reading for your child who has a mental disability or if they are in a coma type situation. Still, before giving the reading, you should always meditate first and ask their Higher Self. If the child is old enough to understand, then before doing the reading you should ask permission. The only reason this is an exception is that you are the guardian of your child. Once they reach an age of understanding, you need to allow them to choose for themselves and respect their privacy even if they are your child, *unless you feel they are in danger in any way.* You'll have to use your discernment carefully in this case.

That is the only exception. For every other situation with every other person, you should ask permission. Unethical behavior like reading for people without permission is not good for you or anyone in the long run. You don't want any more Karma on your plate!

Not only does asking for verbal permission to read someone's Records help you to maintain your integrity, but it also helps the person you want to heal and read. That person needs to be with you as you do the reading for the healing to go deep and completely release what is not serving them. The best healing happens when the person involved takes personal responsibility, sees their part in it and can then feel the connection to their highest potential. By asking if you can read for them, you are helping others to take personal responsibility for their choices.

However, if you want to read for a new girlfriend or your father that you hate, I suggest you stop yourself. The emotional attachment that you have with them will not allow you to give an ethical reading. But remember: what you can do instead is go into your own Records and see how *you* relate to *them* or look at your relationship Records. In any relationship, you are there to work on your issues, and you will be able to learn and heal so much that it may change your relationship with that person completely. Working through your relationships by looking within yourself will also help you to grow, no matter what happens with the other person.

There have been times when I'm in the Records, and I receive information about a relationship or a situation even if I didn't ask specifically about it or ask permission. I trust the Records, and I know that if I see the information, it is for the best of the person I'm reading for and their relationships.

YOUR INTENTION & BEST PRACTICES

Setting an intention before giving readings to others will help you proceed in the most positive frame of mind. You will give even better readings this way, and it will help you to avoid some common pitfalls. Your biggest intention is to be of service and to be a clear channel of information. Affirm that for yourself every time you give a reading. This section will help you do just that.

I suggest at the beginning of learning to give Akashic Records readings for others when you are starting out, try to enjoy the process and see where it goes. Ask family and friends if they would like a reading and have fun with it. I like to tell my Intuitive Development classes that a good attitude to have is to treat readings as a game. It's ego that gets in the way of a clear reading. When the ego thinks you are just having fun and you are playing, it has a lot less to say and doesn't get too involved.

If you want to help others, be conscious of any judgments that you have about them. As you live your life and before you give a reading, these judgments may be swirling in your mind, making you feel emotional. Judgment, anger or any negative feelings are not good when you are working in the Records. They will get in the way, especially when reading for others and you could provide distorted information. Clear and cleanse your energy first before giving a reading or entering the Records. If you are not sure how to do that you can go to melissafeick.com/sacred-chakra-training/ and download my chakra cleansing meditations and make sure you clear the clutter in your head as I explained in Chapter Four. The clearer your energy is, the better your readings will be.

Before reading for others, it's also important that you have spent time in the Records exploring and working on yourself. The more familiar you are with the process, the better off you will be. You will feel more relaxed, and things will come to you more easily. There will be some people that will dive right in and start reading for themselves and others, while other people will take their time. Don't worry about it. There is no right or wrong way for you. Trust yourself. All your Spiritual Council asks is that you try. Your higher guidance has already led you to the Records—there must be a reason you are here devouring this book! As a student of different healing modalities, personally, I tend to jump in and start working on people, this is why my spiritual guidance is so strong. The Masters know that I will usually follow through on information. They are asking you to follow through too. Don't let the ego's fear drag you down and hold you hostage. Trust in your guidance and go for it! You won't know what you can do until you try, be clear on your intention and take the next step that feels right for you.

Remember that no one is perfect and you still have an ego. Sometimes people feel drawn to give readings or healings for ego-related reasons. The Records are not to be used to control or try to get someone to do what you want them to do! Connecting to the Akashic Records is a sacred experience, and you are privileged to be able to access them. In the past, people had to use very specific rituals and ways to open the Records. Within the past several years, I have had strong guidance to go back into the Records. That was when I received guidance to go deeper. All the information in this book then came to me, and I was Divinely guided to show others how to access the highest Akashic Records. To many people in the spiritual community, this information will be brand new. It didn't use to be this easy! Appreciate what a sacred gift it is every time you access the Records, especially if you have the honor to do this for another person. When you are in the process of reading for another person, let go of what the information means for you, or what you will gain, and focus on them.

When you access the Records on the Emotional and lower Mental planes, there are different rules and regulations. The Records on the Quantum Field have a different energy, and they are always open for you to read. That's what makes this information different to anything else you may have read so far, and why it is so important to have a clear intention to be of service, permission from your client and a clear slate internally so you don't add mental judgments or your own emotions to the mix. You'll have a clearer line to the Quantum Field and the transformations possible there. I find that when my intention is to be of service, I lose my judgments and the information flows easily while in the Records.

Everything you do in the Records is sacred and should remain confidential. You may want to tell your clients this before you begin or even have it in writing. Any information the client tells you as you go through the process, as well as what you see within the Records, is just for your client or to help you to serve them better. Ethically, you wouldn't want to share that information and reveal the client's identity with anyone else. When you read the Records, it is important to be of the highest integrity. You can explain this to your clients if you choose.

STEPS TO ACCESSING AND READING A CLIENT'S AKASHIC RECORDS

The steps to give a reading to a client are very similar to giving yourself a reading, with a few changes. Be sure to be familiar with the steps as laid out in Chapter Nine. Once you are comfortable reading your own Records, you will find it simple to start reading for others.

The best part of doing Akashic Records readings for yourself and others is that there is an opportunity for healing throughout the session. Many times the healing is happening later in the reading, during the unwinding process, but sometimes it happens instantly, as soon as you access the Records. How and when the healing happens is between the person receiving the reading and healing and the frequency of their Records.

1. Before the first session or reading

Ask the client to be in a quiet place so they can be open and receptive to the information. You can do the reading over the phone, skype, online or in person. You can record the reading if you would like.

Have the client prepare for your meeting by writing down a few detailed questions they want to ask. I try to guide them toward asking about family patterns, relationships or their professional life. The Records are there for insight and healing. You may need to educate the client about the purpose of the reading and how questions asked should be for deep purposes. It is a much deeper and more profound kind of reading and experience.

The Records are vast (infinite, really) and the more detailed the questions are, the easier it will be to connect with the information that they want. If they ask something broad like, "What about my relationship?", then you may have lifetimes of information flooding in. The client has had many relationships just in this lifetime! They had a relationship with their friends, coworkers, parents, pets, the swim coach they had for six years, their favorite teacher, and so on. When they state what they want to know, ask them to be as specific as possible with names and situations. You're not asking for a detailed report, just enough to get to the correct Records.[8]

Make an intention to read for a specific amount of time. When you are starting out, start with a 30-minute reading and see how it goes, but of course, there are no hard rules here, just steps to guide you.

2. Clear your thought forms and activate and align your chakras

Your next intention is to do the meditation to clear your thought forms and activate and align your chakras. I feel this is an important step, so you are ready to connect to the Records and help your clients receive the deepest healing.

Once the thought forms clear and the chakras are activated and aligned, you should feel your heart expand and become the Toroidal Field around your body. It is a moving vortex of energy and, when activated, it opens up your consciousness and helps you connect to the Akashic Records. This coherence also allows your ego to take a back seat while you are in the Records and makes everything flow more easily.

---

[8] If you would like a basic list of questions your clients can ask please go to https://melissafeick.com/akashic-records-questions/

3. Ask permission

You will not be able to access the Akashic Records of someone without their permission, as stated before in this chapter. When someone asks you to read for them, that means they have given you their permission. Now tell the client that you will be quiet for a few minutes while you connect to their Records. Once you've done this a few times, you may get to the Records very quickly!

4. Intention

As you connect to the Records, start with an overall intention. You can say this out loud or state it in your mind. Making an intention is the easiest way to keep your focus and to get the best results. Your intention when going to another's Records should go something like this:

"My intention is to access the records of *Name*, to be of service and to be a clear channel of information to help them in the highest and best way. I surrender and relax into the Records and allow the wisdom of their Spiritual Council to lead me to what is in the best interest of *Name*."

This is just a suggestion; you may use this script or whatever intention is best for you.

5. Relax your body

You are just going to close your eyes and take a few deep breaths and allow your body to relax.

6. Expand your consciousness into the Akashic Records

Your intention here is to expand past the Physical, Emotional and Mental planes into the Akashic Records on the Quantum Field.

Once you cohere in Step Two (above), you want to feel the heart center and allow it to expand out and become aware of your whole energy field as a toroidal field. You are expanding your consciousness. You want to expand your consciousness because your consciousness has unlimited energy and can easily become one with the Universe and the Quantum Field. Your consciousness has done this thousand of times.

Being cohered during this process (Step Two) is essential since the ego mind will have less to say and your higher consciousness will follow the path it knows well.

You are expanding past your physical bodies into the Universe, past the stars and planets into the Emotional Plane, into the Mental Plane, and then beyond these, into the Akashic Records on the Quantum Field. (this is the meditation in Chapter 2)

You know you are there when you feel expanded, you don't see anything, and you feel calm. If you are questioning if you are there or not, start all over again and cohere and expand. The ego is the only part of you that questions. Your soul or higher consciousness knows where it's going and what it's doing. So if you find yourself doubting, keep working on the foundational steps above.

7. Ask your client their first question

Ask your client what their first question is. Once he or she asks a question, the information will start to unfold around you. You will start to feel and sense the emotions and the story connected to the question, which will usually come to you in an instant download of information. Take a breath if you feel unsure where to start, sometimes this can be a lot. Hopefully, the specific nature of the question they prepared (as stated above) will help you to hone in on what is most relevant to begin explaining. You want to explain to your client what you are feeling, sensing and experiencing to give them clarity on the question asked.

This is their reading and experience. Be open to what is happening and how they respond so that you can be as clear as possible and help them to understand.

8. Unwind the Emotions and Patterns

Give the client all the information about every aspect of what's happening in the Records. Once the feelings, Karmic patterns and mental images come up, explain what these are (how you sense them) and ask the client if they are ready to release the patterns. Your intention is to help them unwind their Karmic patterns and the old stuck emotions surrounding their problems. Throughout the reading check in with the client and ask, "Does this make sense?" or "Do you need clarification?" Often, the healing starts to happen organically, without much thought or action.

The best healing happens when the client takes responsibility for their actions or feelings. If the client comes to you blaming other people, they may not be ready to take responsibility during the session, but let them know that they do have power. The Records will always reflect this, so it may require some courage at times to share exactly what the Records say, but it will plant a seed for the client even if they need time to take it all in. Keep going over every aspect until you feel it resolved and the reading for that question feels complete.

You can ask for a sign from the Akashic Records when you are complete within that part of the Records. For me I know we are finished when:

- I hear the word 'Complete.'

- The Records move away from what I was working on and moves in a new direction.

- I feel like there is nothing else to do.

You can also ask the Records to give you a specific symbol to signify completion like a red light.

9. Highest Potential

The Records hold your Karma, and they also have access to your highest potential. That is the higher state of consciousness of who you truly are. Once your client has received some healing, they are ready to claim the Divine part of them that they have forgotten.

This part of the reading can happen at any time. For me, the flow of a session usually bounces back and forth between this part and sharing information. I will see who they are without all the baggage and Karma. I will see, feel, know and hear amazing things about the client. For example, I will sense things like that they are here to share their gift of Divine compassion or that they are an amazing leader. The Records are there for you to tap into not just what is wrong, but the positive Karma and the truth of the essence of your soul. So you can also do this for all of your clients so that they can see what is possible and what is real: their true essence.

10. Surrender

The surrender part of the healing happens throughout the session. When you relay the information, and the client receives healing and major insight into their Karma, they are ready to let go of how the situation used to be. I ask the client to take a breath and surrender the whole story, emotions, and past back into the Akashic Records. They are taking responsibility for their life, and the surrendering happens once they have set the intention to let it go. The Records have an energetic default that will help this process to happen. Sometimes it just happens organically. Surrendering is so important for your healing, it's not about giving up; it's about letting go of the past and the story.

11. Leaving the Records

Leave the Akashic Records by bringing your energy and awareness back to your heart space. Once in your heart space, cut all energy connections between you and your client.

13. Become aware of the room you are in

Open your eyes and come back to the here and now.

More Information on Reading for Clients

While you are in the Akashic Records reading for your clients, you will experience all sorts of things, so be open to whatever the experience of reading for them may be. You are not there to judge or interpret the information, so voice it even if your ego does not logically understand what you feel called to share. The most exciting part about the Akashic Records is that the information is pretty clear and understandable.

During a reading, you may see your client's feelings, life patterns, Soul Purpose or past lives. You may get a bird's eye view of their Karma or family Karma. You'll connect to any information that is important for their evolution within the Records.

I can't stress enough how important it is to be open and nonjudgmental so that you don't block the reading. You will find it so easy to stay open within the Akashic Records on the level of the Quantum Field, which is the energy of all possibilities.

I want to leave you with encouragement to have fun and enjoy the process of reading for others. Surrender your fears and go for it. You, your clients and the Akashic Records will be thrilled you did!

I did not record the meditation to read the Akashic Records for others, to read for others first practice getting into the Akashic Records and start with reading them for yourself. Next ask friends and family you feel safe with if you can read their Akashic Records, this is a fun, safe way to start reading for others.

CHAPTER 13

AKASHIC RECORDS EXPANDED

GOING DEEPER INTO THE RECORDS

Once you are more comfortable in the Akashic Records and information starts flowing in, you will want to start becoming more inquisitive while in the Records. Digging deeper into the Records as a curious investigator will help you to experience deeper shifts when you're doing your work to heal yourself and when you're reading for others. The information here will give you some guidance while doing readings and healings in the Records.

When you work with the Records, you want to ask good questions. The questions you ask will be more powerful when they are open-ended. Try not to ask questions with yes or no answers because they won't produce the best kind of information. Included in this chapter below is a list of sample questions to get you started.

When you ask your questions, try not to get too emotionally caught up in the answers. Work on becoming an impartial observer while in the

Records. Observing what the Records tell you will help you to get deeper answers and the healings will be more profound.

Although I am giving you an **upgraded method below** and a list of questions, you will find that getting into the energy of inquisitiveness for yourself will serve you well. When you are curious and want to look deeper, and you're interested in knowing more, the questions to ask will naturally come to you.

The best advice I can give is to go into the Records with an open heart and mind. Play with the ideas and healing and don't take anything too seriously. I know healing is a serious business, but you will get the best results when you approach any healing with a childlike imagination, open heart, and belief in miracles!

GAINING WISDOM AND GIFTS

You can also go into the Akashic Records to bring forward wisdom or knowledge. To do that go into the Records and ask the information and wisdom to come through. You can ask to receive anything from how to use a computer program to techniques such as writing a book.

The Records hold all the information so you can access some profound gifts, tools, wisdom, attributes and spiritual tools and gifts. You've been in the Records many times while reading this book and you are just doing the same thing you have done throughout this book. Go into the Akashic Records, make an intention and ask to receive information and knowledge.

When I feel stuck in a project, or I want to start something I've never done before I go into the Records and ask to receive the information I need. Sometimes its given without words and or I am downloaded the information in one moment.

For instance, while writing this book, I would ask to receive the information needed to share the wisdom of the Records easily. I would sit at my computer and the words would flow with little effort from me or I would be downloaded the process.

UPGRADE YOUR HEALING

When you feel stuck and you are ready to take your healing to the next level, or you want to heal a huge pattern you've discovered in your life, you are ready to upgrade the healing potential of the Records. Everything you do in the Records will start to become an organic experience. Please stay open and don't try to overthink anything.

Feeling stuck in old patterns and emotions can be very discouraging. If you feel something isn't clearing in the Records, take some time away and ask your higher consciousness to help you while going about your life. Taking a step back will take the ego's need to control out of the forefront of the problem.

When you feel ready, go back into the Records and do these extra steps but remember, this is an organic process, so allow it to flow.

1. You will want to start the process in Chapter 9.

2. When you get to the place where you feel unsure or stuck:

    a. Know that it can be anywhere in the healing process.

    b. Take a breath and make sure you are in your heart.

3. Ask to see the situation and story differently:

    a. Be open to seeing the situation differently.

    b. Stay in your heart and be the observer without judgment.

    c. Unwind any old trauma patterns that show up.

4. This heals things on the cellular level and rewires the neural pathways in your brain.

The reason this is so life changing is because your past stories of hurt or pain create a whole lifetime of hurt and pain. But these are just stories. I have heard thousands of stories from people and, to be honest, they all start sounding the same. While you are in the Records, you will notice that all these lifetimes of stories are the same story with different characters. Take your power back from the difficult stories and start living the story of unconditional Love, inner peace, and Joyful bliss!

QUESTIONS TO ASK FOR SELF-HEALING WHILE IN THE AKASHIC RECORDS

The questions and list below are just ideas and are in no way a complete list. Please feel free to add to the lists or change anything to suit your needs.

You will ask lots of questions while you are working in the Records.

- How is this pattern like my family patterns?

- How did I feel?

- Where did this Karmic pattern or Karmic tie originate?

- What can I learn?

- What else do I need to know to experience the deepest healing?

- What is the benefit of this pattern?

- What do I get out of having this in my life/relationships?

- When did this begin for me?

- What was the traumatic trigger that started this pattern?

- How has this pattern affected my family?

- How has this pattern affected my relationships?

QUESTIONS TO ASK FOR OTHERS WHILE IN THE AKASHIC RECORDS

You will want to ask the same questions above, and since you are already in their Records you will get the answers for them!

PATTERNS TO PAY ATTENTION TO WHILE IN THE AKASHIC RECORDS

When you are in the Records, pay attention to the energy. If it feels very heavy or stuck, explore whether or not it is part of a larger pattern. Below are examples of possible patterns. They can also be a focus for you if you'd like to go into the Records and intentionally clear these different energy patterns one by one, or whatever calls to you for healing.

Theme/Patterns

- Sacrifice
- Sacrifice Part of Yourself
- Martyr
- Prove yourself
- Lack of authenticity
- Against family policy or belief system
- Family shame
- Betrayal
- Abuse (Physical/Mental/Emotional/Sexual/Spiritual)
- Addiction
- Grief
- Abandonment
- Guilt

- Victim
- Chaos
- Ego Power
- Self-Righteous
- Physical/Emotional/Mental Ailments
- Prejudice
- Lack
- Perseverance
- Lack of financial freedom

Possible Gifts You'll Discover While in the Records

You came here with gifts, and they can be very diverse. We wouldn't want everyone to be a great artist or musician. While you are in the Akashic Records, ask what gifts are innate within you. Most likely there are quite a few of them, so stay open to the possibilities. One interesting gift I have seen in a few people is the gift of connection. These people can connect people together; they will say, "You should talk to Sally, I feel you, and she can help each other." My point here is that some gifts are usually not what humans would call gifts. Please be open and allow that information to flow.

Again, this list is not complete. It is just a starting point. Be open and available to what the Records are showing you.

Gifts

- Ability to Connect People Together
- Seeing the Truth
- Seeing Beyond the Illusion
- Having an Open Heart (Even if it's not open now.)
- Relaying Information with Ease
- Understanding Human Beings

- Comprehending the Larger Purpose of Things
- Seeing the Patterns in the World
- How Energy Operates
- Connecting with Others Intimately
- Understanding How Things are Organized
- Ability to Lead Others

Notice none of these gifts is a vocation. You have come here to express these gifts, but it doesn't matter how you do that. For instance, you could have the gift of *Comprehending the Larger Purpose of Things,* and you could decide to express it through a corporate business, while another person might choose to express it by being an advocate for the environment. In both of these examples, you work very different jobs, but both of you use your gifts to do your jobs.

Another example of this is the gift of *Connecting with Others Intimately.* One person may express this through writing poetry, and another may express it by being a healer. They both make people feel safe, and they both utilize the gift of intimacy to connect.

Some people don't understand or allow these gifts to be present in their life. They have too much trauma, Karma, and ego to express them completely. You will want to work in the Records and transcend as much of your Karmic patterns as possible, so you naturally start to fully express your gifts.

When you no longer live in your past, you feel Oneness and bliss. You'll be able to express your gifts. You will be astonished how new experiences and opportunities will be more available to you!

Chapter 14

Master Your Life
and Raise Your Vibration

There is a phrase I have often heard, which is, "Honey, you are only human." It's true. You are human, you exist in a human body, and you are experiencing existence on the Earth Plane. You may not, yet, be at the highest vibration that you could be but the potential is there. You are human, and you are a light being, connected to the Divine. You have the potential to develop abilities beyond what most people call normal like telepathy and intuition.

Writing this book has been a pleasure. The information contained within the Akashic Records can drastically change your life, especially since the energy is multidimensional. All along, the material that you have been reading connects you to the Akashic Records on the Quantum Field. The energy of the Records work on you even when you are reading the book, so you do not just absorb the material mentally, you absorb it energetically.

My intention is to help you transcend your Karma and embrace more of who you are. Then after you create those inner changes, you can see big changes happening in your physical life, as well. I have tried to explain the simple, yet complex relationship between how to transcend the lower experiences and feelings so that you can create the life you desire. Each concept I relayed is a part of this, like Karma, ego, illusion, Soul Purpose and self-realization.

I want to help you understand the interaction of these concepts and how they all work together to help you transcend the lower vibrations and ego self. They work together to help you connect to the energy of your higher consciousness, like self-Love, Inner Peace, blissful Joy, and Oneness.

When you incarnate here on Earth, you come into a very dense reality, but that is only part of it. You are also from the animal world, and that means you have animal reactions like fight, flight, freeze, and hide. The animal reaction is part of the ego and the ego's drive to survive. The key to your existence here is to override those animal instincts with your higher consciousness. It will take you out of reactionary mode into Oneness mode.

So, your Karmic patterns and ego fuel these instinctual reactions and the illusion keeps them stuck in your everyday experiences. Then these reactions become a habit and you start reacting to minor events like your life depends on it. The work you do in the Akashic Records will help you recognize these reactionary patterns and transcend them.

The way to transcend is to become more aware of the illusion of the world and your unconscious reactions. Most of the time you are reacting from a default in your subconscious, which means you are unaware of what you are doing to create your reality before you go through the motions. When operating on this subconscious, instinctive level, most people don't ever even realize the full meaning of their actions even after the fact. They feel their behavior or response was justified, and this is where self-realization comes in! When you are more aware of what's happening and of the connection to your Soul-self, Karmic patterns, your animal nature and the illusion, you start to transcend the ego self.

So your Soul Purpose on this plane is to transcend the Karmic patterns that you've been working through lifetime after lifetime. You chose to come here to transcend the Karmic patterns. These patterns create experiences and opportunities to overcome or transcend. You incarnate here with the purpose to transcend your Karma, but then you start to believe in and get caught in the illusion of this world. You start to believe that what you see and hear is real and that you are a victim of the circumstances. You believe you don't have any control over what happens to you. The only way to overcome this false belief is self-realization.

With this newfound realization, you can easily go into the Akashic Records and heal your past by connecting with your Karmic Patterns and your Soul. You will heal and unwind your Karma, see that the story is just an illusion and recreate your story. You'll have the power to reshape your life as your Karma shifts and your old patterns dissipate.

The Records are your connection to the Divine. This connection will serve you for years, as you navigate the Akashic Records to receive healings, gifts, wisdom, and the ability to help others. After all, you are here to master the planes and your bodies, which is easier to do when you are opening up to healings and gifts from the Records. You will achieve your purpose more quickly.

The most life altering aspect of the Records is that you will start changing immediately as soon as you connect to the energy of the Akashic Records on the Quantum Field. You start to change so quickly because the energy of the Quantum Field and the Records *are designed as a transformational tool.*

The depth of the healing you will feel will become deeper and more profound as you continue to work through all your Karma in the

Akashic Records. You'll feel this deep transformation, as you transcend and live in a way that is more connected to your higher consciousness, and then you'll continue to raise your vibration even more.

You may experience natural changes in your life when you transform from those lower vibrations into higher vibrations, like connection, unattachment, and love. You may even notice changes in the people around you, matching you as you grow. You are attracting different situations to you. Some problems may naturally disappear, or new solutions may easily appear instead. It will be easier to make new choices, instead of being stuck in old patterns. Hooray!

Even if you only have a few minutes a day, take the time go into the energy of the Akashic Records on the Quantum Field and be open to the energy. You can also go there during your meditations, and be open to the energy, like Oneness and Divine Creation. Just being in the Records on the Quantum Field can help you transform and raise your vibration.

Everything in this book is helping you reach the higher states of consciousness and master the lower planes and your life. Use the Akashic Records as much as you can to raise your vibration and bring in your higher conscious!

Thank you for reading. Please keep in touch with your transformations, insights, and questions. I know that this book is just the beginning of your journey!

I hope you enjoyed learning about the way that the Records can serve you as a transformational tool. If you would like to become certified as an Akashic Records reader and healer, please go to http://akashicrecordscertification.com and register for an event near you.

Much Love!

Melissa

About the Author

Melissa Feick is the founder of the Spiritual Expansion Academy. She has been studying Metaphysics for most of her life and loves deep conversations and metaphysical connections. Melissa is an Ascension teacher, healer, coach, speaker, and an advanced intuitive. She has been teaching Metaphysical classes for over 20 years and has been an intuitive reader for over 22 years. Her most notable classes are her Akashic Records Certification and her Ascension Workshop.

Melissa lives in Maryland with her family and animals. She is passionate about helping others to raise their vibration, feel more on purpose, and become the power of Joy. She has many online and in-person classes and a fun membership program.

Melissa is available to travel and teach at your location. She is also available for a limited amount of one on one coaching clients. Please contact Melissa at her website below for more information.

Meet Melissa online and receive meditations and trainings at:

https://melissafeick.com/

Also by Melissa Feick

Co-authored

Angel Anthology, Edited by Wendy Gabriel

365 Life Shifts, by Jodi Chapman and Dan Teck

Seminars by Melissa Feick

Akashic Records Certification

Ascension Workshop

Intuitive Development

Sacred Chakra Training

Akashic Records Certification

If you would like to expand your skills within the Akashic Records you may want to join Melissa in her Akashic Records Certification Workshop. In this certification program we will expand on the book and practice Akashic Records Readings on others. I will also teach you how to manifest and heal physical ailments. For a detailed description and to register for the class go to the link below.

http://akashicrecordscertification.com/

Spiritual Expansion Community

Looking for a community of like-minded spiritual seekers? Take a look at Melissa's Spiritual Expansion Academy Community. If you are searching for spiritual answers and a group that understands the difficulties that *empaths, sensitives, and healers* have in this world, the Spiritual Expansion Community is for you!

Welcome to a group where you can talk about everything spiritual, connect with other seekers and feel heard without judgment. As an experienced spiritual teacher, coach and intuitive, I can answer all your questions and support you along your growth path. Good times and bad, through the ups and downs, we're in this together! Go to the link below to sign up today!

https://melissafeick.com/spiritual-expansion-academy-community/

Akashic Records Mp3 Meditations

All the meditations in this book are available as downloadable MP3. Go to the link below to get yours today!

https://melissafeick.com/rar-meditations/

Made in the USA
Monee, IL
23 February 2020